Creating a MASTERPIECE from a MASTER MESS

A "Prescription" to Create an Amazing Life by Igniting Your Inner Millionaire

STEPHANIE E. WILSON-COLEMAN, D.D., PH.D

Creating a Master Piece from a Master Mess
Copyright © 2019 Stephanie E. Wilson-Coleman
The Champagne Connection, Chicago, Illinois
www.champagneconnection.com
www.asipofinspiration.com
Cover design by Borel Graphics
Photographs by SteeleLife Gallery, Chicago, Illinois

All rights Reserved. No part of this book may be reproduced in any form or by any means without permission in writing from the publisher. The Champagne Connection is not responsible or liable in any way for any advice, course of treatment, diagnosis or any other services or products obtained from the website or written materials. All information presented is for general informative purposes only, and not intended as a substitute for professional medical advice, diagnosis or treatment. Never disregard professional medical advice or delay seeking it because of something you have read in my books, articles or on the Champagne Connection website.

The reader should regularly consult a physician in matters related to his/her health and particularly with respect to any symptoms that may require diagnosis or medical attention. Although the author and publisher have made every effort to ensure that the information in this book was correct at press time, the author and publisher do not assume and hereby disclaim any liability to any party for any loss, damage, or disruption caused by errors or omissions, whether such errors or omissions result from negligence, accident, or any other cause.

Some names and identifying details have been changed to protect the privacy of individuals.

Library of Congress Registration Number on file
ISBN: 978-0-9749387-7-6 - Paperback
ISBN: 978-0-9749387-5-2 - Hardback
Printed in the United States

DISCLAIMER

Information and/or practices provided in this book are made available with the understanding that the author nor the publisher do not dispense medical advice nor prescribe the use of any technique as a form of treatment for physical or mental problems without the advice of a physician or health care professional either directly or indirectly.

The intent of the author or the publisher is only to offer information of a general nature to help in your quest for spiritual, emotional and physical wellbeing. In the event you use any of the information in this book for yourself, the author and the publisher assume no responsibility for your actions.

Each person should engage in a health program only in consultation with a physician, therapist or other licensed medical professionals.

DEDICATION

This book is dedicated to my ancestors, for I am standing on the wings of their prayers. To the Divine Intelligence for the Sip of Inspiration I find in my television show, in the lyrics of my favorite song, in the smile of my love ones, and on the face of my enemies. I am grateful to Infinite Kindness, for keeping me, teaching me and guiding me in my endeavors.

May the pages of this book inspire and uplift all who will discover that impossible, simply means I AM POSSIBLE. Know that you are powerful and creative and can overcome any challenge.

Now reach for the STARS.
You Can DO IT.
With the right mindset, nothing is impossible!

ACKNOWLEDGEMENTS

With the help of family, great friends and a lot of prayer, I have learned that our life is a testament that our broken parts, scars, and cracks are an integral part of the recipe of who we are.

I want to thank all of my friends and family who helped me learn to celebrate who I am, "fat thighs and all." (LOL).
Thank you to my parents, who are no longer on the physical plane, but somehow find ways to guide and inspire me.
To my sister, Tonya, and my nieces and nephews who have always shown me love.

To my friends of too many years to mention, Anita, Mae, Edrea, Tre, Charles, Gay, Terisa.

To my new friend, Shannon, who had no idea just how wild my ideas could be.

To my husband, Lester, my son, Karl, and my grandchildren. They inspire me daily.

Thanks to all of you for reminding me that our perfect imperfections is the spice that create our individual brand of awesomeness. Keep it up.

TABLE OF CONTENTS

Recipe.........................vii
Preface........................xi

FORGIVENESS
Prescription #1

The Key to Prosperity – Forgiveness................4
Prescription: Healing My Heart......................4
The Gift of Forgiveness – Richard's Story........19

VISUALIZATION
Prescription #2

When Failure is NOT an Option......................28
What You See IS What You Get........................28
Activating the Law of Attraction....................30
Personal Reflections On Visualization...........38
The Courage to Imagine – Vicky's Story.........40

STAYING IN THE MOMENT
Prescription #3

The Art of Living in the Now.........................50
The Staying in the Moment Formula..............51
Five Senses Exercise....................................52
Finding the Power – Carolyn's Story..............53

STOP HOSTING PITY PARTIES
Prescription #4

The 80/20 Rule...64
Money Drama to Financial Responsibility.....67
Embracing Your Awesomeness–
Helena's story...69

PLAN TO SUCCEED
Prescription #5

Fast Track Your Plan to Succeed....................80
Feelings – A Matter of the Heart...................81
Goals Require Action..................................87
Taking Action to Succeed – Noah's Story........91

GRATITUDE:
The Fuel Necessary to Live Your Dreams

The Fuel Necessary to Live Your Dreams......102
Steps to Take..103
Gratitude Journal......................................104
Rampage of Appreciation............................105
Ending the Struggle with Gratitude –
William's Story..110

Conclusion 115
Epilogue 121
Resources........................123
Notes 143
Appendix 153
About the Author. 161

Creating a MASTERPIECE from a MASTER MESS

2 cups of Visualization
Sharpen your vision of who you are
and what you want to accomplish.
Then work to make your life a living legend.

1 ½ cups of Planning to Suceed
Ben Franklin said well done is
better than well said.
Frequently look at your actions
to determine if you are on track.

1 cup of Staying in the Moment
Because there is a lot of activity
between the asking and the receiving,
commit to spending one uninterrupted
hour daily working your dreams.

1 cup of Gratitude
Each experience is our creation;
develop the habit of celebrating
everything in your life.

10 Oz of Tithing
Because we are all one,
when we give to each
other we are giving to ourselves.

4 heaping cups of
Spiritual Understanding/Forgiveness:
Make it your goal to forgive and forget
the pain associated with the event.

1 lb of Good Vibrations
Our seeming successes
and failures are filled with
many miracles and blessings.

Life is too short to drink cheap champagne

There are an endless number of discoveries, daily, uncovering techniques and practices that will help us live the lives we were created to live.

My goal in this book was to put into one place the techniques and practices that I used to change my life.

Let's Sip into Something Inspiration.

Stephanie E. Wilson-Coleman, Ph.D.,
The Empowerment Doctor

It matters not how strait the gate,
How charged with punishments the scroll,
I am the master of my fate,
I am the captain of my soul.

    Invictus, William Ernest Henley

PREFACE

My Personal Path to Forgiveness

On one quiet, sunny morning, I found myself filled with so much rage that I wanted to attack everyone in my path. I experienced this level of rage often, since my early teens. I held a lot of hurt and disappointment inside me. I was sexually abused at a very young age, which became a regular occurance. I became a mother at 15. Being stripped of my innocence, forbidden to tell anyone and not believed when I did, invoked explosive hostility. By age 17, any day I did not contemplate suicide was a good day. Because of this rage and the loss of my innocence, I thought if I worked hard and finished first, I could outrun the monsters that never seemed to release me. Finally, the stress of my secret burden and the lack of understanding as to "why" it happened to me, collapsed my life, and despite the successes, I had amassed, I found myself homeless, hopeless, and broken.

By a divine encounter (as I know it to be now), I met a lady who suggested I read *Loving Relationships* by Sondra Ray. In the book, Ray affirms, "If you do not feel undying love for everyone in your life, then you have some work to do on yourself."[1] Being at one of the lowest points of my existence, I decided to try the forgiveness exercises disclosed in the book. After all, what did I have to lose? Gradually I began to learn how to forgive. Since I understood forgiveness would be the first step to my healing, it propelled me to do more and to seek more to forgive and especially to understand that forgiveness was the pathway and requirement to prosperity and physical healing. The feeling of rage began to subside. All this time I thought if I forgave others for what had been done to me that I was giving them a "get out of jail free" card. What I learned was, freeing myself from the past and adhering to my now, allowed me to soar to an unimaginative future.

Moment by moment we are choosing who or what we will serve. When we hold onto any grievance or lack of forgiveness we are binding ourselves to the past. The more we live in the past, the more unlikely we will manifest

PREFACE

the desires of our hearts. Refusing to forgive also guarantees we will create a vibrational alignment with the situation and similar situations will continue to appear in our lives. Forgiveness helps us to resolve the problem at the core, within ourselves, so we no longer create these situations.

The forgiveness process is as easy or as hard as we make it. Forgiveness is absolutely necessary to heal the heart, to heal the soul. Once I stopped labeling events and people as good or bad, I could successfully move through each experience.

Because we are all connected, all of our thoughts and actions affect each other. Once we start to forgive others, and ourselves, our vibration rises, and we are then able to help raise the vibration of others. Each person is our mirror; each moment is our moment of truth. Both serve as bridges to our freedom. Forgiveness opens the path to success. Once we embrace forgiveness, we are able to open our hearts and hear them whisper to us our dreams, which we can then manifest into our physical world.

Remember, life is too short to drink cheap champagne.

Stephanie E. Wilson-Coleman, Ph.D.,
The Empowerment Doctor

FORGIVENESS

Infuse your life with action. Don't wait for it to happen. Make it happen. Make your own future. Make your own hope. Make your own love.

Bradley Whitford

Prescription #1

Shifting my focus from the negative forces that seem to be controlling my life, to the desired outcome, I was able to see solutions that were previously buried under hopelessness.

      Stephanie E. Wilson-Coleman, Ph.D.,
        The Empowerment Doctor

Consultation with
FORGIVENESS

Seeker: But you SAW what THEY did to me! You SAW THEM! Why should I forgive? WHY?!

Forgiveness: Do you believe "they" hurt you?

Seeker: I do!

Forgiveness: Then "they" did. Do you believe that "they" have the power to continue to hurt you?

Seeker: Well, I think they do.

Forgiveness: Then "they" can. Do you wish to believe "they" can continue to hurt you?

Seeker: No. I don't want to do that.

Forgiveness: This is the first step to forgiveness; be WILLING to believe that CHANGING your negative thoughts, seeing that there is no "they" there is only YOU, and you WILL ALWAYS forgive, YOU.

Diagnosis:
The Key to Prosperity – Forgiveness

In my first book, *Is Anybody Listening? A Journey to Wholeness*, I wrote that the most overlooked step is "forgiveness"; everyone, every place and everything must be forgiven. By refusing to totally and completely forgive, you strengthen unfavorable conditions within yourself and guarantee them to resurface. If you still remember the hurt when you recall certain events, you still have some forgiveness work to do.[2]

Prescription: Healing My Heart –
Forgiveness All day, Every day

The new amazing quantum physics discoveries depict the forgiveness process in such a way that it gives room for those who may not be very "spiritual" to understand their thoughts as actions and those actions dictate their transformation. Forgiveness then becomes a means to an end and not some unachievable "God complex" that they can never achieve. The principles are easy to use and have proven beneficial in the lives of those who study this process of thinking and believing.

It has been approximately a decade since the book and the movie, *The Secret*, assisted in transforming minds. This metaphysical phenomenon denoted that one could create all their desires just by changing their thoughts.

> *"It is sometimes said that scientists are unromantic, that their passion to figure out robs the world of beauty and mystery. But is it not stirring to understand how the world actually works — that white light is made of colors, that color is the way we perceive the wavelengths of light, that transparent air reflects light, that in so doing it discriminates among the waves, and that the sky is blue for the same reason that the sunset is red? It does no harm to the romance of the sunset to know a little bit about it."*[3]

Carl Sagan

Dosage:
Ingest your positive thoughts –
Release your negative thoughts

The Secret boasts that "the law of attraction determines the complete order of the universe by creating in our physical world the things we consistently think about." Rhonda Byrne, the author of *The Secret*, says, "our power is in our thoughts and the life we experience is based on the quality of our thoughts."[4] Even though this is an age-old premise, Byrne was able to create a tidal wave throughout the world that resulted in people being willing to accept this as a way of changing their lives. Quantum physicists tell us that "the entire Universe emerged from afterthought" and because all thoughts are composed of vibrational matter you can *THINK* your life into existence.

Thus, as defined in the Metaphysical Dictionary, the basics of forgiveness is a process of giving up the false for the true or erasing sin and error from the mind; giving power to those wishing to change their lives to "**ask, believe and receive.**"

As an introduction to the aspect of forgiveness as prosperity, healing, and happiness, I like to have those wishing to transform their lives understand more about their thoughts and how those thoughts become **things**. If one's "thing" is material prosperity and they are trying to understand more about why they do not have the car, the house, financial success, etc., then we address the forgiveness aspect of their requests and usually discover they are harboring bad energetic thoughts toward those who have money and prosperity. One cannot receive what one is not willing for others to receive. **Forgiveness deems that one cannot receive what one is not giving and vice versa.**

Follow up appointment #1:
Fear, Finances, and Forgiveness

In this high-tech, low-tech society, one sentiment is echoed throughout the media, "the rich are getting richer, and the poor are getting poorer." What is keeping many from following the philosophical wave of "change your thoughts, change your world?" What do so many really believe?

In September 2011, Baylor University published "The Values and Beliefs of the American Public" report. This research revealed that approximately 73% of Americans believe that God has a plan for them and 87.9% believe that anything is possible if they work hard.[5] Really?

How does the ordinary person, with no trust fund and a bad credit rating create true wealth? How do you know what God's plan is for you? If hard work and religion are not the keys to wealth, then what is? If we believe we are made in God's image and likeness, what is 99% of the population sowing? Why is it that only 1% of the population knows about creating wealth and the rest of the population or more than 70% of Christians do not? And, if most people are always working just to meet basic expenses, then when is there time to feed the soul? What is that 99% harboring that prevents them from receiving the "trickle-down economics" prosperity? Does NOT forgiving the rich for being rich, keep the poor, POOR?

In *Wealth Inequality in America*, author Politizane pointed out that 1% of the population owns 40% of the U.S. wealth and half of the country's stocks, bonds, and mutual funds, while the bottom 80% owns only 7 % percent of America's wealth.[6] In a 2016 Gallup report, the Americans Financial Worries Edge Up article revealed that nearly 60% of Americans **fear** their ability to afford retirement, pay for unexpected medical costs, and maintain their standard of living.

FEAR stands in the way of the 99% understanding that their backlash toward those who are rich, who they think are robbing them of their wealth, is why they cannot rise above their poverty. **What is the remedy?**

In 2016, According to the Bureau of Labor Statistics (BLS), 62.8% of Americans were actively employed. A suggestion like "Success is the result of perfection, hard work, learning from failure, loyalty and persistence," (Colin Powell) strengthen Americans belief that the answer to equalize the distribution of wealth in America is based solely on hard work and not their thoughts. The BLS report also indicates that hard work alone is not the key to wealth.[7]

In *A Course in Miracles*, Lesson 16, **I have no neutral thoughts**, says that "besides recognizing that thoughts are never idle, salvation requires that you also recognize that every thought you have brings either peace or war; either love or fear. A neutral result is impossible because a neutral thought is impossible." If the majority of the population is living with thoughts of fear regarding finances, how are we masking this fear so successfully that we are unaware of the creative ideas that are tugging at our hearts and souls? **In other words, what has our attention and where have we placed our energy?**

This is where the "aha!" moment begins for everyone wishing to improve their finances and place themselves in a forgiveness position, so to speak, to receive the benefits of being free of fear.

Economists Todd Hirsch and Robert Roach explain, "Economic wealth is not created by oil and gas molecules in the ground, or by an auto assembly plant. It is not created by tax credits or subsidies. It is not even created by economic development programs. Wealth starts with one thing: **an idea**. What's powering those economies are not resources, necessarily, but applications of creative ideas."[8]

Albert Einstein also believed that creative ideas or the imagination is the key to achieving great things. "Imagination is more important than knowledge." he states.

A silver-haired woman calling herself, Peace Pilgrim, who walked more than 25,000 miles on a personal pilgrimage for peace said, "If you realized how powerful your thoughts are, you would never think a defeatist or negative thought."[9]

Since wealth is created by an **idea**, having an active, awakened imagination is key to creating success and wealth in our lives regardless of any current circumstances. This will normalize the wealth distribution in the United States. We can clean the slate of our circumstances as forgiveness lights the path to prosperity.

Forgiveness:
Follow up appointment #2

Colin C. Tipping, author of *Radical Forgiveness: Making Room for the Miracle*, gives us step-by-step instructions on what begins as a healing process and culminates in an entirely new way of living in the world. You will discover how to transform difficult emotions like anger, fear, and resentment into unconditional love, gratitude and peace. Explore the five essential stages of *Radical Forgiveness* and how they help us transcend the victim archetype and embrace the inherent perfection of life. And put it all into practice with the tools of *Radical Forgiveness*, a series of quick, effective and easy-to-use techniques. This book is particularly helpful for the person new to even understanding their need for forgiving. It is cohesive and easy to read and the teachings will lead one toward forgiveness. [10]

Forgiveness Pharmacy Location:
Faith

We are instructed to bless others, tithe 10% of our income and that we reap what we sow. Forgiveness verses are also abundant in the Christian faith, and many passages point to the "whys and what fors" of forgiveness for the believer. We find many examples of this in the Holy Bible, King James Version **(KJV)**:

> "And be ye kind one to another, tenderhearted, forgiving one another, even as God for Christ's sake hath forgiven you." Ephesians 4:32

> "And when ye stand praying, forgive, if ye have ought against any: that your Father also which is in heaven may forgive you your trespasses." Mark 11:25

> "If we confess our sins, He is faithful and just to forgive us [our] sins, and to cleanse us from all unrighteousness." 1 John 1:9

> "But if ye forgive not men their trespasses, neither will your Father forgive your trespasses." Matthew 6:15

> "Then came Peter to him, and said, Lord, how oft shall my brother sin against me, and I forgive him? till seven times?" Matthew 18:21-22

> "For if ye forgive men their trespasses, your heavenly Father will also forgive you." Matthew 6:14-15

The New International Version (**NIV**) includes verses with similar translations.

> "For if you forgive men when they sin against you, your heavenly Father will also forgive you. But if you do not forgive men their sins, your Father will not forgive your sins." Matthew 6:14-15

> "When you are praying, first forgive anyone you are holding a grudge against, so that your Father in heaven will forgive your sins, too." Mark 11:25

Forgiveness:
Preventive medicine

Thomas C. Corley, the author of *Rich Habits*, sums it up by stating that the difference between the wealthy and the poor are their habits. Corley identifies the number one habit that will create wealth is to limit daily television viewing to one hour.[11] The Nielsen Total Audience Report, Q2, 2017, revealed that Americans watch an average of 6.1 hours of television daily while, according to Corley, the rich adhere to one-hour. *What do happy people do?* Authors John Robinson and Steven Martin, at the University of Maryland, conducted a 30-year study between 1975 and 2006 and found that unhappy people watched significantly more television in their spare time.[12]

People who need a financial awakening have been lulled into trading an additional 5 hours a day or 35 hours a week for entertainment, as opposed to achieving wealth. Most people are watching television shows that range from *The Real Housewives* to *Keeping up with the Kardashians*; from *American Idol* to the *Walking Dead*. With the aid of television, the idea that you must be rich to experience the best life has to offer, or you will end up as a dead man walking, talented, but a zombie nonetheless seems to have left people believing the rich must possess something magical. **People are using television to self-medicate.**

Blocking the ability for the mind to receive the messages of the heart through mindless "entertainment" and excessive television viewing must be brought to the forefront for those who are having problems with prosperity and forgiveness. The vicarious nature of man to "live the life" of those presented on the screen can inhibit one's search for prosperity and health and keep the continuous flame of blame burning which will surely stop and prohibit prosperity in all things.

In other words, cut off the TUBE!

Forgiveness Pharmacy Location:
Your mind

Dr. Paul Leon Masters reminds us that prosperity is a state of mind in which one experiences happiness and peace within and about oneself. He further states that prosperity is not only financial, it also includes love, health and happiness. Experiencing one of these elements without the others is not true prosperity. The mind must experience prosperity in all areas of life.

In his book, *Think and Grow Rich*, Napoleon Hill states, "If you do not see great riches in your imagination, you will never see them in your bank balance."[13]

The problem is not rich or poor, nor is it tied to racial identity. The problem is being in the flow.

Roger G. Lanphear, author of *Wealth Consciousness: A Guide from Babaji for Prosperity* says, "The flow represents all of creation, and just by being in the flow, we touch each and every aspect of creation. That is why abundance and wealth come to us when we are flowing." He also says that "the lingering feelings we get when we think someone has hurt us is similar to anger. Left to fester, it surely interferes with our flow of wealth. The remedy is simply forgiveness, although most of us would resist forgiving."[14]

Start with Forgiveness -
Heal Your Heart.

The *Merriam-Webster Dictionary* defines forgiveness as "to give up resentment of or claim to requital for; to cease to feel resentment against." It has been proven by a myriad of medical professionals including Dr. Steven Standiford, Chief of Surgery at the Cancer Treatment Centers of America, Dr. Peter Breggin, Master Charles Cannon and Will Wilkinson that unforgiveness is deadly. Un-forgiveness has been linked to cancer, depression, high blood pressure, frustration and even self-hatred. If you are experiencing any type of dis-ease and pain, it may be because you are not on the path of forgiveness.

Carolyn Myss, author of *Entering The Castle,* says the reason for our refusal to forgive is because of our unreadiness. "I am not ready to be compassionate toward everyone. I still need to feel superior to others in order for me to keep my world in order." A passage in *Entering The Castle* sums it up nicely, "Being judgmental of others and holding on to negative thoughts blocks the emergence of mystical love. You cannot be bitter or unforgiving and be a conduit for love and grace. Heal your heart. Allow it to give up old wounds."[15]

Forgiveness is often a concept that is very difficult to grasp and at times more difficult to understand and consistently put into action than tithing. Forgiveness is not about forgetting the event occurred; it is about refusing to re-live the pain of the past.

Forgiveness lifts our vibration to attract more of the universal Goodness.

Consultation:
Bad Things that won't go away

Seeker: I don't know. It is like I live under a dark cloud, it's always raining and it just follows me.

Things: But we are all you think about. Darkness and sadness.

Seeker: Really? I never thought of that.

Things: We are permanent until YOU decide to think of something besides us.

Seeker: How do I stop thinking about bad THINGS?

Things: Start by healing your heart!

Diagnosis:
Can't See Life Changing for the Better

Once we have forgiven the hurt and harm others have caused us, we may find that this is not enough. In the Holman Christian Standard Bible, King Solomon said, *"Above all else, guard thy heart; for out of it flow the issues of life," Proverbs 4:23.* King Solomon equated life's problems as an "issue of life" and all solutions to life's problems must begin with healing the heart.

Scientists have discovered a phenomenon called "Cellular Memory." Dr. Eric Nestler M.D., Ph.D., Nash Family Professor of Neuroscience and Director of the Friedman Brian Institute at Mount Sinai states, "Diseases that show up later in life could be due to negative memories programmed into cells as you age. Cancer can be considered the result of bad cellular memories replacing good ones. Psychological trauma, addiction and depression may all be linked to such abnormal memories inside cells." Dr. Robert Rodgers, Ph.D. says, "these thoughts that nurture the [unhealthy] symptoms have to be released, removed, detached, ejected and shielded before the body will return to its natural state of balance, clarity, centeredness and overall health. As long as these thoughts remain, you are cultivating a garden of low frequencies that promote ill health." Dr. Bruce Lipton, the author of *The Biology of Belief*, said, "We react based on our perception of the environment and not as it really is. Genes and DNA do not control our biology, DNA is controlled by signals from outside the cell, including the energetic messages emanating from our thoughts."[16] The science of genetic memory or epigenetics supports Carl Jung's theories that "racial memories are posited memories, feelings and ideas inherited from our ancestors as part of a 'collective unconscious.'"

These memories are filled with thoughts and beliefs in poverty, lack or limitation, generations will continue to manifest according to this innate belief. Healing the issues of the heart must include healing the beliefs and experiences that have been generationally passed down to all through the cellular memory.

Prescription:
Techniques for Healing Cellular Memories
Healing My Heart: A Personal Memory

Years ago, when I was temporarily homeless, I realized I had a tremendous amount of knowledge, but it was a mystery as to why everything I tried ended up a financial disaster. The more I learned, the more I tried. Napoleon Hill says that both poverty and riches are offspring of the same thought. Someone once asked Warren Buffett how he would describe the difference between getting rich and being wealthy. His answer was short and to the point; "People seeking riches never have enough. Wealth is a state of mind. Wealthy people always have enough."My constant vacillation between ideas and principles kept me stuck between poverty and riches. My laser-like focus on creating money clogged my state of mind and kept me vibrationally attached to more debt, so I went back to the basics, and I rediscovered several key principles or laws that helped me end the struggle with poverty, by creating a state of mind that attracted true abundance. Daily I strive to live the definition of true abundance by first finding peace and happiness within myself, which requires me to start with forgiveness so I can heal my heart. A return to the basics included forgiveness, healing my heart and cellular memories. This resulted in me saying YES to love, saying YES to financial success. The results continue to amaze me.

"My first serious attempt at forgiveness occurred after I was jarred from a peaceful nap by a presence so haunting that I was unable to go back to sleep. Suddenly, I found myself in my teenage body filled with intolerable pain that resulted from sexual molestation and surrounded by people telling me that I was not worthy. The longer these emotions lingered, I came to realize that they were shaped from things I was never allowed to talk about or share with others. Fearful that these little secrets had the power to ruin my life, a life that was finally filled with some success, I tried forgiveness. I used a simple technique. For 21 days, three times daily, I looked into a mirror and said, "I forgive any person, place or thing that has caused me harm, hurt or injury. I release you to your highest good." I had no idea where I learned this statement, but it worked. That pain, those memories have never returned."

Life will present forgiveness opportunities. Refusing to heal your heart will keep you from establishing a mental equivalent for the success we all crave. If you are experiencing any problems, especially financial problems, you have some forgiveness to do.

Forgiveness allows one to believe the dreams in their hearts and the magic they can create; to feed only the thoughts that inspire and the wisdom to ignore the rest; to surround oneself with people who motivate and create like-minded circumstances. Finally, peace and a calming of my spirit led me to understand how wonderful life is when forgiveness of others becomes a part of the spirit's equation. Each person is our mirror; each moment is our moment of truth. Both serve as bridges to our freedom.

In the magic of this moment, with a healed heart, trust Spirit, your intuitive guide, with the manifestation of all your desires, dreams and prosperity. Allow forgiveness to quiet the turbulent waters in your life, to lead you to green pastures and restore your soul.

> *When you hold resentment toward another, you are bound to that person or condition by an emotional link that is stronger than steel. Forgiveness is the only way to dissolve that link and get free.*
>
> **Catherine Ponder**

Dosage:
Make the decision to be HAPPY - Heal Your Heart

Because there are a lot of techniques available at no cost and are easy to practice, try as many as possible to find the ones that work best for you. I have used the Energy Medicine Tool by Dr. Alexander Lloyd and have found it to be quite helpful.

The Energy Medicine Tool, by Dr. Alexander Loyd, from *The Love Code: The Secret Principle to Achieving Success in Life, Love, and Happiness*, states that everything in the body works on energy; every cell, thought and feeling. **The Heart Position** pours energy into your cardiovascular system and thymus. The cardiovascular system, which is 100 times stronger than the brain, governs all of the control mechanisms, including the mind and spirit. **The Forehead Position** stimulates your entire brain and governs your feelings, beliefs, actions, images and the Third Eye. The last position, the Crown Position, known as the **Top of the Head Position**, activates your crown chakra and spinal column that provides powerful energy medicine to your spiritual realm.[17] A condensed version of Dr. Alexander Loyd's Energy Medicine Tool process is below.

Position 1:
The Heart

In the first position, you place one hand (either left or right), palm down, on your upper chest (over your heart), and place your other hand, also palm down, over the first.

For this position and for the others that follow, you have two options: you can either rest your hands in this position and hold for one to three minutes, or you can move your hands gently in a circular motion (clockwise or counterclockwise, whatever is most natural), slowly moving the skin over the bone (not rubbing the skin), switching directions every 15 seconds or so, for one to three minutes.

Position 2:
The Forehead

In the second position, you place one hand (either left or right) over your forehead, with your little finger just beneath your eyebrows (just barely grazing the bridge of the nose), and your other hand on top of that hand, both with palms down.

Position 3:
Top of the Head

For the third position, place one hand (either left or right) on the top of your head, or your crown, and your other hand on top of that hand, both with palms down.

When you apply energy to these three areas—the heart, the forehead, and the top of the head—you're physically increasing blood flow and functionality to the control centers for every cell, every thought, every emotion and every belief, as well as to your heart, third eye and crown chakras, the three most powerful cellular memory energy centers in the body.

Now that you have healed "Your Heart", your vibrational level will increase substantially allowing you to focus on cultivating a mental equivalent that attracts prosperity. Dr. Masters said, "When you begin winning and vibrating to that spirit, life indeed becomes a wonderful game – a game to be lived and enjoyed to the utmost. The "glooms" are no longer a part of your makeup. Time is spent praising life and its rewards, instead of blaming life for its failures."

Follow up appointment 1:

Caroline Myss says, "Where your heart is, there is your power. Without this energy, nothing in your life can manifest or flourish, from your romantic relationships to your artistic creativity."

Using the techniques discussed, opens your heart to love, and love has created professional and financial success. This would not have been possible without forgiveness. Dr. Masters asserts, "Your thoughts correspond to emotional energies that discharge themselves every day through your auric shield." Forgiveness is the salve that clears your heart and opens the doorway to prosperity.

Follow up appointment 2:

During our lifetime, we will live several lives and fill several roles. Each experience will leave its mark; but to really open the door to true freedom and start the journey toward true enlightenment, forgiveness is required. Forgiveness is a gift you give to yourself; it is the necessary ingredient to free your inner spirit and untie you from the past

We have all heard this before; however, sometimes we fail to remember that moment-by-moment we are choosing "whom we will serve." When we hold onto any grievance or lack of forgiveness we are tied to the past, which causes us to serve and nurse old events, old patterns, and old stories.

The Gift of Forgiveness
RICHARD'S STORY

History:

Richard describes mild anxiety related to difficulty with colleagues, whom he describes as un-loyal. He is experiencing difficulty breathing, staying focused, and becomes withdrawn at home. Richard denies any thought of harm toward himself or others. His best attempt to relieve the symptoms was to work late into the evening which has resulted in feelings of fatigue due to lack of sleep.

Sessions:

From the outside looking in, Richard had a perfect life, a family that loved him. His wife adored him, and his children looked forward to spending as much time with him as they could. He had a job that paid enough to ensure his family was well supported.

After experiencing an "encounter" at work that felt hostile, Richard started to experience shortness of breath and believed his colleagues were deliberated trying to derail his career and destroy his reputation.

Richard contacted me to discuss these issues with someone who could be objective; someone he could talk to, and to help him sort this out.

I gently suggested he contact a medical professional, because this seemed to be beyond the realm of my expertise. I explained that I provided "Holistic Counseling" which deals with Spiritual issues, and not trained or equipped to handle "medical" issues. Robert insisted that he believed I could help him sort through "things." I also secured his promise that he would also seek medical help.

During our sessions, we focused on the "feelings" that surfaced during his "encounter" and were able to trace them back to several instances where he was the victim of childhood bullying.

few sessions, Richard also began to remember instances of sexual molestations. Because my life experience included sexual molestation, I incorporated some of the spiritual techniques that were successful in my life. Reminding Richard of his promise to see medical professional help, we proceeded.

Forgiveness techniques from The Castle by Caroline Myss are intense, so we worked this technique. We made great progress as we worked forgiveness techniques for everyone who had harmed him. We then included exercises for forgiving himself.

Within 30 days, Richard did visit his medical professional. His health was great, he was sleeping better, and has received a " surprise" promotion.

For maintenance, I prescribed a "Forgiveness Pill" to be taken 3 times daily.

Easy Action Steps for Adding "Forgiveness" to Your Spiritual Practice

- Set aside 2-5 minutes a day. You're going to make two list.
- List # 1 - Make a list of the people or events that you need to forgive. Did someone of something upset you? Hurt you? If so, add the person or thing on your list.
- List # 2 - Make a list of people or events where **you** made someone anger.
- Say this quick prayer:

    - Anyone that has caused me harm I forgive you and release you to your highest good. Anyone that I have cause harm, I ask that you forgive me.

    - Also forgiving yourself is a very crucial element. Now say aloud, I forgive myself. You forgive yourself. Thank you Divine Light (or any word you use when referring to a "Higher Power" or "God"). We are forgiven and surrounded by the healing power of the Divine Light.

That's it. I recommend you do this daily. You will be surprised by the number of painful events we hold on to.

FORGIVENESS

VISUALIZATION

"Sincere forgiveness isn't colored with expectations that the other person apologize or change. Don't worry whether or not they finally understand you. Love them and release them. Life feeds back truth to people in its own way and time-just like it does for you and me."

Sara Paddison

Prescription #2

Then the LORD answered me and said: "Record the vision and inscribe it on tablets, that the one who reads it may run. For the vision is yet for the appointed time; It hastens toward the goal and it will not fail. Though it tarries, wait for it; For it will certainly come, it will not delay.

Habakkuk 2:2-3 (NASB)

Consultation with
VISUALIZATION

Seeker: All I **see** around me is failure.

Visualization: Is that ALL you **see**?

Seeker: Most of the time.

Visualization: Do you ever **look** for anything else?

Seeker: I never thought about it.

Visualization: Exactly.

Diagnosis:
When Failure is NOT an Option

In today's world of technology, we are overloaded with information. Every news media outlet seems to dwell on information regarding crime, poverty and, of course, the rich and famous. Crime seems to easily link to poverty but little information is shared about how to eliminate poverty and create wealth, especially under extreme stress or trauma at a young age.

The media often reports that a life with these elements is designed to fail. TalkPoverty.org, a project implemented by the Center for American Progress, reports, in its Basic Statistics section, that in 2015 there were 100.9 million people or 31.7% falling below the poverty line in the United States. In 2016 the overall poverty was 13.5% percent or 43.1 million people living in poverty.

With the media's intense messaging on hopelessness coupled with our willingness to accept it, the question is, are we comfortable with our bondage, with our predetermined failure? Failure must NOT be an option.

Prescription:
What You See IS What You Get

"A solitary fantasy can transform a million realities."
Maya Angelou

Everyone has a dream of something they really want. Something that makes your heart skip a beat just thinking about it. Do you have a dream that is so extravagant, extremely beautiful, immensely opulent and extraordinary, that the thought of it leaves you breathless? Take a few seconds to close your eyes and visualize that it is yours. You can almost touch it, taste it, see it, and feel it. Now open your eyes. Unfortunately, for most people, the reality of their present situation dissipates their glorious dream when they open their eyes. Merging positive thoughts into a dream will enable the dreamer to manifest their dream. **Thinking** defined is to, have in the mind; have as an expectation; to form a mental picture of. This is the key to manifestation in its purest form.

Visualization is Faith in Action

Man has received mandates regarding this readily available tool of thinking throughout many religious formats. *"After these things the word of the Lord came unto Abram in a vision saying, Fear not, Abram: I am thy shield, and thy exceeding great reward." Genesis 15:1* **(KJV)**. Abram's fear came from an "idea" of which a "vision" of the Lord requesting him to have faith appeared. Thus the formula, of Visualization equals Faith in Action, can be applied. **Thinking and seeing...**

Dr. Paul Masters states, "Inside of your mind right at this moment are ideas that can bring you life's richest rewards. All it takes is one good creative idea to surface into your conscious mind, and you are on your way to greatly improving your life." One idea, one spark of brilliance surfaces and life can produce the wildest of dreams, the fondest of dreams. It might depend on the perception of "reality."

Eric Butterworth, the author of *Spiritual Economics*, affirms, "Your perception is shaped according to your faith, according to where you are in consciousness. When something is awry in your life... when you understand the law of visualization, you will realize the greatest need is to not set it right but to see it right."[1] In essence, "seeing it right" could mean a change of reality, or seeing the thing desired as something that is, even though it is not currently present. The paradox of understanding faith has always eluded even the most conscious of those among us and in some cases, many who have trouble accepting the realization of their dreams as "faith" or a denotation of religion. The option of science or physics has served to bring a greater acceptance of manifesting one's dreams.

TruthUnity.com metaphysically defines "faith" as, "the perceiving power of the mind-linked with the power to shape substance; substance is the living energy behind all things." With the scientific discovery of the Non-Locality Theory or the wave/particle duality, Physicist David Bohm concluded that everything in our universal plane is interconnected and made of energy. Scientists have also agreed that we have the undeniable ability to choose how we will respond to the events or dramas in our lives and this action serves as some sort of a conductor to attract items with the same vibration to us. Without what may be perceived as the limitations of religion, accepting connectivity to vibrations is what Michael Brown, author of *Finding the Field: an Adventure of Body, Mind, and Spirit*, calls the Third Universal Truth. Brown states on his website, "The third universal truth is that all things—seen and unseen—are connected. All things are different faces of consciousness. The Field, the Great Spirit, the Source, the Tao, the One, are all names for the same thing. The universe is consciousness and creates whatever object you can name—a mountain, a mouse, a fish or a fowl, a blade of grass or a puff of air—all of it is consciousness

Dosage:
Activate the Law of Visualization

Scientists have researched, discussed and documented the art of visualization for years. However, it was only when some fairly well known, non-scientific people publicly confessed that it was this practice that helped them achieve their success. Listed below are a few of these non-scientist visualization super-stars:[2]

- Carli Lloyd - U.S. women's soccer team's star player credits visualization with helping her during the 2015 FIFA Women's World Cup where she was named the FIFA World Player of the Year. While training just before the game, Lloyd said she mentally visualized herself scoring four goals. She later went on to nail three into the net—the first woman in World Cup history to do so. It's as simple as turning on the radio and tuning into the right frequency.
- Jim Carrey – In the early 1990s, Carrey was an unknown actor struggling to get by. To stay motivated, he decided

VISUALIZATION

to write himself a check for $10 million for, **acting services rendered**, with a 1994 date. He carried it in his wallet for daily inspiration. In 1994, Carrey learned he would reap exactly $10 million for his role in Dumb and Dumber. Today, Carrey is one of America's top movie stars, and he credits his constant visualiz-ation with helping him get there.

- Arnold Schwarzenegger said, "It is one thing to idolize heroes. It is quite another to visualize yourself in their place. When I saw great people, I said to myself, 'I can be there.'"
- Oprah Winfrey, the multi-faceted media mogul who became one of the world's wealthiest people said, "Create the highest, grandest vision possible for your life, because you become what you believe."
- Lindsay Vonn articulated, "I always visualize the run before I do it. By the time I get to the start gate, I've run that race 100 times already in my head, picturing how I'll take the turn."
- Will Smith affirming how the visualization techniques helped him along the way stated, "In my mind, I've always been an A-list Hollywood superstar. Y'all just didn't know yet."

https://www.brainyquote.com/quotes/quotes/w/willsmith167218.html

The use of visualization, creative or otherwise, is the answer to living your best life. No matter what you desire, this is a key to that success. If you want to achieve fame, wealth, excellent health and more, this is an essential process. So how do others who do not have any "stardom" harness this readily available mechanism? Dr. Masters provides the following guidelines for visualization in his curriculum. There is also a process used by many others.

CREATING A MASTERPIECE FROM A MASTER MESS

- Form a mental picture of what you wish to materialize in your life.
- See this mental picture in its completed state.
- Hold this mental picture in your mind in its completed state until it is completely materialized in your physical life.
- Discuss what you are trying to materialize with as few people as possible. Talk about it only to those who are directly involved in its materialization. Avoid discussion with friends and relatives.
- Plan everything that you do in your life to revolve around the materialization of your desire.
- Do not let your attention be diverted.

Make a commitment to view your mental images several times daily. Sustained visualization will soften your resistance and increase your vibration toward your dream. Once you are able to hold this positive vibration, you will be able to taste, touch and experience the thing that you see so vividly. Neville Goddard, Metaphysical Practitioner, says, "Determined imagination, thinking from the end, is the beginning of all miracles."[3]

Often we feel the process of visualization, as described above, seems too simple and on the first few attempts we start to wonder if this will work. We ask ourselves if we are confident enough or believe deeply enough to vision ourselves into success. Living in your imagination is easier than you think; there is no requirement to eradicate anything you are currently experiencing. The requirement is to shift your focus to what you would like to experience. As you spend more time living in your imagination, you automatically decrease the time you spend "living in your nightmares." The research performed by M. Jeannerod has "successfully proven that motor images are endowed with the same properties as those of the (corresponding) motor representation and therefore have the same functional relationship to the imaged or represented movement."

Follow Up Appointment #1

Most people take for granted the ability to visualize. If seeing is believing, what if you are one of those people who cannot visualize? What if you suffer from a little-known condition called Aphantasia (the inability to visualize), which was first identified by Sir Francis Galton in 1880? Then try imagining.[4]

Dr. Alexander Berzin, in his column, *Visualization Means Working with the Imagination*, believes that Western Civilization must broaden its view of visualization. Berzin says, "It is the wrong word because the word *visualization* implies something visual ... we must work with our imagination which allows us to work with imagined sights, sounds, smells, physical sensations, feelings. We do that with our minds, not with our eyes. Tibetan Buddhism develops both sides – both the intellectual, rational side and the side of creative imagination ... allowing us to deal with creativity, artistic aspects and so on." If you have difficulty visualizing, the popular website Brain Rules states, "people are incredible at remembering pictures. Hear a piece of information, and three days later you'll remember 10% of it. Add a picture and you'll remember 65%."[5] So if you are having trouble using visualization, try creating a Mind Movie, visualization filled with pictures.

Mind Movies began when a factory worker in Sydney, Australia decided to make a simple 3-minute slideshow that was uploaded to YouTube. The factory worker, who remains anonymous, partnered with Natalie and Glen Ledwell to create Mind Movies.

The Mind Movie:
Visualizing through Technology

To create a Mind Movie, you will need a few tools, which are easily accessible with a computer, laptop or smartphone. Some tools are listed below and can often be used at no charge.

For PC's, Microsoft PowerPoint is available with the Microsoft Suite.

PowerPoint will allow you to save the file as a slide show or a video. For Mac computers, Keynote and iMovie are available at no charge. Both can be used to create movies.

After the software has been chosen, follow the steps below and create a Mind Movie:

> **Step 1**: Write the script. When writing the script, it may help to think about the following areas: Home/Physical Environment; Career; Fun; Money; Personal Growth; Spiritual Growth; Health; Romance; and Family and Friends.
>
> **Step 2**: Find pictures that identify with your interests. Search the internet to find more pictures; there is an abundance.
>
> **Step 3**: Add the pictures to the software and save as a video and/or slide show.

If quieting the mind and getting still is problematic, you can try "Drawing Your Vision" into reality.

Patti Dobrowolski answers the question, "So how can you use a picture to get what you want?" Simply draw one! You don't have to be an artist or know how to draw. As simple as your drawings might be, when you draw where you are, your current state, and where you want to be, your desired new reality, you surprisingly have a roadmap for change.[7]

Here are the steps to drawing your future from Drawing Solutions:

> - **Step 1** – take a sheet of paper and divide it into three (3) sections.
> - **Step 2** – Label the sections as follows: Left side – Current Realty; Middle - 3 **Bold Steps**; Right Side – **Desired New Reality**. For your current reality ask yourself: What does it feel like to be living my life right now? What is the

state of my finances, relationships, health and spiritual life? For your desired new reality, ask yourself: In the best case scenario, if all goes well and everything works out just perfectly, what will my life look like and feel like one year from today?

- **Step 3** – On the left side draw a picture that depicts your current reality. On the right side draw pictures that depict your desired new reality.
- **Step 4** – Under the 3 Bold Steps section, write down the ideas that come to mind. Now highlight the three steps on your list that are bold steps. Step one should be something that you have been keeping inside, like "quit my job or stop smoking."

The second step should require you to change your immediate environment like "get serious about my health," and the third step should be self-reflective and more personal like "step out of my comfort zone."

Visit her website for more info:
https://upyourcreativegenius.com/

Remember that everything will not unfold as drawn or imagined but the things desired will become real.

Follow Up Appointment #2
Mindful Seeing

For those who are unable to create images in their mind, or who are dissatisfied with the way images are processed by their mind, may find Mindful Seeing helpful.[8]

Mindful Seeing is a relatively simple exercise requiring access to a window view, or at a minimum, the ability to see the outdoors. It's recommended that the exercise be conducted by a facilitator using the following steps:

- **Step 1:** Position yourself near a window or any other mechanism that allows you to see outdoors.
- **Step 2:** While gazing outdoors, take your time to look at everything within your sight noting everything you can about what you see. Do your best to avoid labeling or judging what you see. Focus on the attributes only, such as color, texture and how you think it may feel.
- **Step 3:** View what you see as if you needed to describe it to someone who has never seen it before. Pay attention to any wind, grass, flowers or trees.
- **Step 4:** Observe the scene without becoming fixated on any one particular thing. Practice being in the moment.
- **Step 5:** If you find your mind thinking about something other than what you see outdoors, refocus your mind by noticing something else in your view.

Pharmacy Location: Self-Inquiry Meditation

The Self-Inquiry Meditation, as outlined and defined in the Positive Psychology Program, "is focused on self-inquiry, a technique used in meditation to gain enlightenment."

You start the Self-Inquiry Meditation by first identifying the area in which you want to focus. You can choose a particular part of your body, a thought, a feeling. If you are unable to decide where to place your focus, ask out loud "where do I need to place my focus?" Follow the guidance you receive. Keeping a record of the Self-Inquiry Meditation sessions is recommended but not mandatory, however, recording the experience will help you remember how powerful the sessions are and the benefits you receive from each session.

VISUALIZATION

To begin the exercise, follow these steps:

Step 1: Get into a comfortable seated position.

Step 2: Take a few minutes to allow your mind and body to settle into a relaxed state.

Step 3: As you continue to relax both your mind and body, clear your mind of any thoughts. As you relax you may find it difficult to completely clear your mind, but do not allow this to distract you. Dismiss the thoughts and continue to relax and clear your mind. You may have to do this several times.

Step 4: Focus your attention on the feeling of being you. Who are you? How does it feel to be you? What is it that makes up your inner self?

The Program states, "The goal of self-inquiry is to be aware of yourself and to bring awareness to the source of all that you are. It can be so easy to get lost in everyday tasks and distractions."

Simply stated, the process of visualization can be summed up as faith in action. We must diligently guard where we place our faith.

The universe is more interested in moment-to-moment decisions and visions. Visualization, as it is often practiced, is physical, but in order for lives to change, visualization must become spiritual. It's stated in the textbook of *A Course in Miracles*, "the world you see is what you gave it, nothing more than that. As a man thinketh, so does he perceive, therefore, see not to change the world, but choose to change your mind about the world."

> *"Having seen and felt the end,*
> *you have willed the means to the realization of the end."*
> **Thomas Troward**

Personal Reflections On Visualization

Several years ago, my aunt sent me a book by Catherine Ponder, *Dynamic Laws of Prosperity*. I was intrigued by the principles presented and decided to test them. As I began to practice the principles gratitude, visualization, staying in the moment, and transforming the tendency to focus on the negative, my life began to change in ways that seemed magical. With no further convincing necessary, I had discovered the missing elements. The more I integrated metaphysical spiritual principles into my life, the faster things changed for the better.

Amazed at what I could accomplish in, what seemed like, a few hours, I continued to explore spiritual principles on abundance and discovered that **Visualization** – *imagining your success;* **Staying in the Moment** – *your only point or power;* **Stop Hosting Pity Parties** – *what you focus on is what you create;* **Plan to Succeed** – *developing sound principles for handling money;* and **Gratitude** – *focusing on what you have to be grateful for; along* with **Forgiveness** – are key to creating prosperity.

Mark 11:24 **(KJV)** tells us to, pray believing that we have received it and it will be ours. And Luke 12:32 **(KJV)**, reminds us that *"it is the Father's good pleasure to give us the kingdom."* All religious texts advocate the principle that God, the Living One, says yes to our beliefs. With this in mind, the most important work we can do is to uncover our true beliefs and rid our subconscious of all limiting, poverty-filled thoughts.

VISUALIZATION

A common religious saying is "speak the word, name it and claim it," however, this is never followed up with practical steps for manifestation. Embracing these steps will help one unbind from the bondage of poverty and lack so that freedom, abundance, and prosperity can materialize.

Life is too short to drink cheap champagne.
Stephanie E. Wilson-Coleman, Ph.D.,
The Empowerment Doctor

The Courage to Imagine – Visualization in Action
VICKY'S STORY

History:

Vicky R, extremely educated and successful by everyday standards, is stuck in the belief that she lacks the ability to achieve her definition of success. While she has achieved success, she strongly desires to move up the corporate ladder. Everything she tries has backfired. She had difficulty believing that she was worthy of success. In her own words, "who would hire a woman my age?" Vicky was fixated on the thought that she would not achieve the success she craved. She was "stuck" in this failure, and applied it to every area of her life. And now, Vicky was sabotaging every opportunity to move forward.

Sessions:

Throughout the sessions, Vicky quickly pointed out her shortcomings in every situation. In order to gently change her refocus, I had her create a "Brag List" that included 5 things she has accomplished that she was extremely proud of. Her list was amazing. She also assigned a word to each item on the list to help her remember them. Her instructions were simple:

- Read them twice a day, once in the morning and again before she went to bed;
- Carry this list in her purse every day.

This activity resulted in redirecting Vicky's focus, however, she needed more. Any event would cause her to focus on the areas of her life that were not working.

Deciding that is was time for a little fun, we amped up the assignments. Vicky's homework was to create a "Mind Movie" using the steps below:

- Using any computer software, and Vicky had access to many, Vicky was tasked to:

VISUALIZATION

Step 1: Write a script for as many areas of life as possible. It was mandatory to include Career; Fun; Money; Personal Growth; Spiritual Growth; Romance; Family/Friends.

Step 2: Find pictures that identify with these interests. I recommended using magazines. Vicky needed to see more images of success.

Step 3: Add the pictures to the software and music.

Step 4: Save as a video and/or slide show.

Prescription:

Watch the Video every day for the next 21 days.

What you see is what you get, so it was imperative that Vicky begins to see "success" as often as possible.

Vicky reported that by demanding she see and visualizes success, she was able to see herself doing what she really loved and got that promotion.

Easy Action Steps to add Visualization to Your Spiritual Practice by Visualizing Using Your Senses

Think of something you would like to accomplish. Limit this to one item. Too many items may distract your focus.

What do I SEE?
What things are present? What is my view? What else do I see? (decor, etc).

Use some of the suggestion below to capture the images
- Pinterest Board.
- Dream Board (Vision) using magazine images.
- 3X5 Index cards - list your goals and keep in your purse or pocket.
- Crystal Grid.
- Feng Shui.
- Screen Saver - computer phone.
- Sand Mandala.

If you have additional ideas, feel free to use them

What do I HEAR?
Who's talking or cheering? What white noise do you hear, machines, etc?

Use some of the suggestion below to capture the audio
- Record short audio memos about how it feels living your dreams.
- Talk about your goals with your accountability partner.
- Role play you being interviewed by your favorite talk show host, news personality.
- Practice your acceptance speech for receiving achievement awards.
- Use words like ... doing, I am moving forward. Avoid "going to do".

VISUALIZATION

Where is my VIBRATIONAL level?

List the "WHYS" for achieving your goals.

List the reasons why you cannot achieve your goals.

Use Energy Clearing Technique to raise your vibrational level - a few are listed below

- EFT - Emotional Freedom Tapping
- Violet Flame energy
- Cutting the Spiritual Cord
- Chakra Balancing
- Sacral Cranial Healing Therapy
- NLP - Neuro Linguistic Programming

What do I FEEL?

Where are you sitting? What's the temperature? What are you wearing?

What do I TASTE?

Is there food? What's in the air? What on your lips, mouth?

What do I SMELL?

What in the air? Do you smell perfumes, creams? Are there any odors? Using one, several or all of them will help you to create a strong image of what you would like to accomplish.

Just for today, keep your mind filled with possibilities not obstacles. Trust that Power greater than yourself to guide and direct your steps. Keep your conversations filled with the good you deserve and watch this goodness engulf you.

Just for today, believe that the Universal power is working to shape your world in ways that you cannot begin to imagine.

Just for today, nothing will be impossible.

**Stephanie E. Wilson-Coleman, Ph.D.,
The Empowerment Doctor**

VISUALIZATION

Staying In The Moment

Prescription #3

"The future is ahead, prepare for it. The present is here, live it. If you want to conquer the anxiety of life, live in the moment, live in the breath."

Amit Ray

Consultation with
STAYING IN THE MOMENT

Seeker: Well, IT all happened many years ago.

The Moment: What happened?

Seeker: Everything that is wrong with me today.

The Moment: But you said it happened many years ago.

Seeker: IT did!!

The Moment: What does that have to do with TODAY?

Seeker: Nothing I guess

The Moment: Breathe. Just breathe.

Diagnosis:
The Art of Living in the Now

"We live in the age of distraction. Yet one of life's sharpest paradoxes is that your brightest future hinges on your ability to pay attention to the present."

Jay Dixit

Eckhart Tolle says in *The Power of Now*, "the only place where you can experience the flow of life is the Now, so to surrender is to accept the present moment unconditionally and without reservation. In the state of surrender, you see very clearly what needs to be done, and you take action, doing one thing at a time and focusing on one thing at a time. Learn from nature: See how everything gets accomplished and how the miracle of life unfolds without dissatisfaction or unhappiness." Even though Tolle demonstrates the power of living in the present moment throughout his book, Susan Nolen-Hoeksema's research reveals that a percentage of people are caught up in a cycle of over-thinking situations or life's events. This leads to dysphoria, and dysphoric participants focused on troubling problems, family conflicts, and financial woes. The participants constantly retrace past mistakes and conjure up more negative thoughts. They become trapped on the endless hamster wheel. Self-reflection is a technique recommended to improve this situation.[1]

In 1979, Buddhist MIT trained molecular biologist, Jon Kabat-Zinn, was determined to introduce to the American western culture the benefits of the Buddhist meditation practice. At the University of Massachusetts Medical Center, Kabat-Zinn created an outpatient program in Behavioral Medicine for chronic pain patients, based on the practice of mindfulness meditation. Mindfulness is one of the two major classes of meditation practices that could be easily introduced. The primary focus of the program was to measure levels of pain. The process consisted of the patients observing their thoughts and to treat all thoughts as equal while not becoming involved in the individual thoughts. After the last cycle of meditation, 21 out of 36 (57%) patients reported a 33% decrease in pain and 12 out of 37 (32%) reported a 50% or greater reduction in pain over 10 weeks. Even though the reduction in pain was impressive, the unexpected results of non-pain symptoms were outstanding. The group reported large decreases in negative mood disorders, such as depression, tension and anxiety, and an increase in energy.[2]

Prescription:
The Staying in the Moment Formula

In 2012, researchers Simon Gregoire, Therese Bouffard and Carole Vezeau confirmed that individuals who are more attentive and concerned are more actively involved in the achievement of personal goals. An individual who actively and consistently practices mindfulness tends to be more focused when it comes to achieving personal goals. The researchers also recognized that the "participants with higher mindfulness scores reported more autonomous personal goals than those with lower mindfulness scores and suggested that mindfulness brings clarity to actions.[3]"

A new study found that "94 percent of people have unwanted, intrusive thoughts and impulses," and according to the San Diego Supercomputer Center (SDSC) at the University of California, San Diego, we consume 6.9 million-million gigabytes of information or a daily consumption of nine DVDs worth of data per person per day.

Dr. Paul Leon Masters said, "Do not contaminate the psychic atmosphere with negative thoughts. Each thought is telepathic. Each is magnetic. Each thought builds an atmosphere of conditions and circumstances in your life."

With the improvement of the non-pain related issues demonstrated by Jon Kabat-Zinn, we know that by simply observing and not judging a thought prohibits the thought from energetically drawing like thoughts into your life. So how does one stay in the moment with so much data competing for time? Don't let negative thoughts, which have built up during your day, be taken to bed with you at night. Proceed to eliminate them from your mind.

During a 10-part series presented on Oprah's Super Soul Sunday, Tolle shared two simple techniques for staying in the moment:

1. Ask yourself, Am I still breathing? You will suddenly feel the air flowing into and out of your body... At that moment, you've entered the state of presence. Even if it's only five seconds.
2. Use all your senses when going through habitual, everyday motions, such as washing your hands. "Do it consciously," Tolle instructs. For example, [when] you wash your hands; feel the water. Smell the soap. Becoming acutely conscious of sense perception means looking, hearing, touching. It brings you into the present moment.

These exercises may take a little effort at first, but Tolle says that they do eventually become second nature. "The more you bring those moments of presence into your life, the more your old conditioning becomes eroded, gradually. Your mental atmosphere or state of mind is the key."

Dosage:
Five Senses Exercise

This five senses exercise provides guidelines on practicing mindfulness quickly in nearly any situation. All that is needed is to notice something connected to experiences with each of the five senses:

- **Notice five things that you can see.**
  Look around you and bring your attention to five things that you can see. Pick something that you don't normally notice, like a shadow or a small crack in the concrete.
- **Notice four things that you can feel.**
  Bring awareness to four things that you are currently feeling, like the texture of your pants, the feeling of

the breeze on your skin or the smooth surface of a table you are resting your hands on.

- **Notice three things you can hear.**
Take a moment to listen, and note three things that you hear in the background. This can be the chirp of a bird, the hum of the refrigerator, or the faint sounds of traffic from a nearby road.

- **Notice two things you can smell.**
Bring your awareness to smells that you usually filter out, whether they're pleasant or unpleasant.
Perhaps the breeze is carrying a whiff of pine trees, if you're outside, or the smell of a fast food restaurant across the street.

- **Notice one thing you can taste.**
Focus on one thing that you can taste right now, in this moment. You can take a sip of a drink, chew a piece of gum, eat something, notice the current taste in your mouth or open your mouth to search the air for a taste.[4]

Follow Up Appointment #1

If you only have a minute or two or, for whatever reason, you don't have the time or tools to try a body scan or fill out a worksheet; the five senses exercise can help you bring awareness to the current moment in a short amount of time.

This quote by Dr. Masters outlines an effective, simple technique:

> "When alone and reacting negatively to your own thoughts say, 'Every thought I am now thinking is a SIGNAL in my mind to have negativity sublimated to positiveness that fills my mind from the wisdom of spiritual understanding flowing into me from my higher God-mind.'" This can be used throughout the day as an affirmation.

Follow up appointment #2

As the mind is trained to live in the moment we will realize that "we are not our feelings. We are not our moods. We are not even our thoughts," Steven R. Covey. This sanctions the understanding that there is so much more.

In his book, *The Power of Now*, Tolle states, "that's why Jesus said: Look at the lilies, how they grow; they neither toil nor spin." If your current circumstances are unbearable, switching your focus to what is good, no matter how limited, will improve your state of consciousness and cause the things that are unbearable to disappear. When you no longer resist, you are no longer a vibration match to unpleasantness, causing it to transform into an experience that matches your new vibrational level.

Finding the Power of Being Present
CAROLYN'S STORY

History:

Carolyn P. had one problem. She thought this was a "small, little" thing. Carolyn has a habit of comparing every event to something that happened in the past. She projected the failure of past events onto future events. Carolyn was stuck and refused to move forward because she knew she would fail. Otherwise, she was healthy. She contacted me to help her work through this issue.

Sessions:

I tasked Carolyn with bringing her focus to the present by using a combination of popular techniques.

At a specific time of day, Carolyn would do the following. Because Carolyn was an early riser, we decided on 5:00 AM.

Interrogating thoughts of the past:

What? When? Why?
Write down each feeling about the past event.
What did you learn?
What will you do differently in the future if this event re-occurred?
How has this helped you make better decisions?
Re-write the story as a Mystery.

Finding the Magic in the Moment:

In order to help her find the magic in the present moment, I prescribed the Self Inquiry Exercise.

To begin the exercise, follow these steps:

CREATING A MASTERPIECE FROM A MASTER MESS

1. Take a comfortable seated position.
2. Let yourself settle into your body and your mind.
3. Try to let go of thoughts and clear the mind of its usual considerations.
4. Focus your attention on the feeling of being you. Who are you? How does it feel to be you? What is it that makes up your inner self?

If you find yourself distracted by an errant thought, bring your awareness back to yourself by asking "To whom is this thought occurring?"

Within 21 days, Carolyn was able to stay more focused on the good that was occurring in her life.

Easy Action Steps to add "Staying in the Moment" to Your Spiritual Practice

- Set an hourly reminder to 'pause' your activity for about 30-60 seconds and focus on your breath.
- Next, quickly survey your body for any pain, tension, or soreness. Focus on each area where you feel stress for about 5 seconds and give the command to "relax".
- Smile.
- Practice listening to your surroundings. How many different sounds to you hear?

Choose to think beyond the boundaries of your past life.

Stephanie E. Wilson-Coleman, Ph.D.,
The Empowerment Doctor

STAYING IN THE MOMENT

STOP HOSTING PITY PARTIES

Prescription #4

*If you keep telling the same, sad, small story,
you will keep living the same, sad, small life.*

Jean Houston

Consultation with
PITY PARTIES

Seeker: Oh, whoa is me!

Pity: So True!

Seeker: Nobody cares about me!

Pity: No they don't!

Seeker: Why are you agreeing with my pain?

Pity: What does that have to do with TODAY?

Seeker: Because it is what you KEEP believing!

Seeker: That makes me so sad!

Pity: Yep, you are…

Diagnosis: The 80/20 Rule

The true test of one's faith and conviction is not when all is well, and calmness is apparent in every direction, and everything touched turns to gold. The true test is when, like the children of Israel, being chased by Pharaoh's armies into an ocean filled with uncertainty and darkness, your sight becomes limited, revealing no way to turn, no way out.

Some people experience more adversity than others, but when any real adversity shows up in our lives, we diligently call our card-carrying Pity Party buddies to recap all of the terrible events. We quickly decide who is to blame, never looking inward for the answer. After we have become fearful and discouraged, we collapse into utter despair. Dr. Susan A. Everson-Ross completed a study that found that people who reported high levels of hopelessness or despair had a 20 percent greater increase in hardening of blood vessels. This is equal to the same risk as a pack-a-day smoker to a non-smoker.

Dale Carnegie said, "feeling sorry for yourself and your present condition, is not only a waste of energy but the worst habit you could possibly have.¹" Dr. Everson-Ross has also proven that it is bad for your health. According to Dr. Masters, "What you believe about yourself is affecting you mentally, emotionally, spiritually and physically – more than anything else in life that you meet, for the greatest encounter in life is when man comes face-to-face with himself."

Prescription:

An old Cherokee is teaching his grandson about life. "A fight is going on inside me," he said to the boy. "It is a terrible fight and it is between two wolves. One is evil – he is anger, envy, sorrow, regret, greed, arrogance, self-pity, guilt, resentment, inferiority, lies, false pride, superiority and ego. The other is good – he is joy, peace, love, hope, serenity, humility, kindness, benevolence, empathy, generosity, truth, compassion, and faith. The same fight is going on inside you – and inside every other person, too." The grandson thought about it for a minute and then asked his grandfather, "Which wolf will win?" The old Cherokee simply replied, "the one you feed." Knowing which "wolf" to feed hinges on being able to recognize the behaviors.

TinyBuddha.com offers the following observations to know if one is seeking pity:

- Frequently starts sentences with "I didn't deserve..."
- Regularly tells others that life or parts of your life are unfair.
- Repeatedly talks about how someone has harmed you.
- Draw attention to your problems and ask why they had to happen to you.
- Subtly wish for negative outcomes so you can talk about them.
- Get caught up in your own head and become unaware of other people.
- Look at someone else's misfortune through how it negatively impacts you.

The Loner Wolf also offers ways to know if one is seeking pity because they:

- Find it hard to laugh at life and at themselves;
- Tend to crave drama.
- Tend to crave sympathy.
- Tend to be an individualist.
- Tend to be a past-oriented person.
- Have low self-esteem.
- Have a melancholic temperament.

- Don't believe you're worthy of love.
- Have an unhealthy habit of being self-absorbed.
- Have a strong fighting instinct.
- Subconsciously feel guilty.

To feed the wolf that is **good**, stop hosting pity parties. Stop talking about problems; the universe is listening. A person can never rise above the level of their conversations.

Prescription:
Remember the 80/20 Rule always!

Believe in the saying, "80% of the people don't care, and 20% of the people are glad it's you." No matter what is going wrong in your life, stop talking about it. When one talks about what is wrong with their life, they are actually focusing on about 20% of their life. Dr. Masters says "what appears to be negative is always a blessing in disguise – one that will cause you to do things differently, which, in the final analysis, will result in greater good in your life."

Deliberately shift your focus from injustices to blessings for which to be grateful. Stop talking about your problems because they are a mirror; they exist in life to introduce one to oneself and to tell how something in that life needs to be changed.

Dosage:
Check your associations

Look for the win-win in life. Stop associating with "pitiful" people. People who are always complaining, always sad and never have a good thing to talk about. To change your life you will need to change your playground, playmates or playthings. When an unpleasant situation materializes, it is packed with information, so ask the simple question "what am I to learn from this?" If one quiets the mind, the situation will speak.

Follow Up Appointment #1

The May 2015 issue of Forbes.com listed additional ways to feed the good wolf:

- Face Your Feelings – allow yourself to experience the emotions.
- Recognize Warning Signs of the Downward Spiral - When you focus on everything that is going wrong in your life, your thoughts become exaggeratedly negative.
- Question Your Perceptions - Mentally strong people question whether their thoughts represent reality.
- Turn Your Negative Thoughts into Behavioral Experiments - don't allow negative thinking to turn into a self-fulfilling prophecy.
- Help Other People - Rather than ruminate on their own inconveniences, mentally strong people strive to improve the lives of others.

Money Drama to Financial Responsibility: A Personal Reflection

My recurring drama was not having enough money. Throughout my life, I seemed to always be faced with financial challenges, because I just never had a sufficient cash flow. I loved shoes and I would spend the grocery money to purchase them. Having misplaced priorities was an understatement. My solution was to figure it out later; I would cross that bridge when I came to it, not realizing that this belief required me to know when I got to the bridge. So, it should not have been a surprise when I found myself homeless. First, I got divorced; next I became unemployed with a whopping $65,000 indebtedness, and finally homelessness. I later realized that my debt was serving as my financial counselor and I could have avoided these consequences had I been paying attention.

I did not expect to be immune from the valley or basement experiences brewing as a result of our race consciousness. I only needed to appreciate the magic in ordinary everyday life. This alone would be enough to be spiritually aligned with the Divine, enough to prove the existence of Spirit in my life and I believe our primary reason for existing is to prove the existence of Spirit in our lives. One can NOW look at the "drama" of their past experiences and transform them into something that can be utilized to realize a better outcome. My life has been filled with hard-hat experiences. To alter my emotions encompassing the events in my life, I demanded myself to think better thoughts. I can achieve better thoughts by consciously deciding to remember only the good from these experiences. The more you practice this technique, the easier it becomes. Following Paul's guidance to think about things that are honest, just, pure and lovely will serve as the bridge from dream to reality. Any improvement in your emotional state will truly be your sip of inspiration. Always look for the **good** in every negative experience. When you are able to do this, your life will improve and you will unknowingly find good things happening."

Embracing Your Awesomeness — Stop Hosting Pity Parties
HELENA'S STORY

History:

Helena was very well educated, petite, and impeccably dressed. She was in a job she loved and paid very well. Helena stated she was here to see me because her husband said she complained constantly and he believed she enjoyed complaining.

Sessions:

Because Helena's educational background was phenomenal, I thought starting with her education, which consisted of 2 master degrees from Ivy League Schools and a PhD., would be a great place. Helena shared that because of her academic performance, she received a lot of scholarships and only incurred a small amount of debt which was promptly paid.

Throughout the sessions, Helena was acutely focused on events that "went wrong" and was upset because it happened to her. Because of this Helena was focused on the 20% of her life that was not perfect instead of the 80% that was going well.

With every experience, Helena complained about the things that were imperfect. When asked what actions she could have taken to improve these instances, she had no ideas and was satisfied with simply complaining about them.

To break this habit, I prescribed the Complaint Jar Exercise and the No-Complaint Bracelet. The rules are similar.

Because Helena was hyper-focused on small mistakes or errors, redirecting her focus to the good that overflowed in her life was essential.

Complaint Jar – Time Period: 60 Days

- If Helena catches herself complaining, Helena is to write the complaint on a sticky note pad (blue) and place in the jar. Her penalty: $1.00 is placed in the jar.

- No gossiping - the same penalty applies.

- If Helena catches herself expressing genuine gratitude, she is to write this on a sticky note pad (yellow). Her reward is to remove $2.00 from the jar.

- Helena must pay attention to how she is speaking. If something happens that causes discomfort, simply make a statement of fact. If she keeps going on and on about the issue, that's probably a complaint. Write the complaint on a sticky note pad (blue) and place in the jar. Penalty: $1.00 is also placed in the jar.

At the end of each 30 day period, review the actions in the jar.

Complaint Bracelet – Time Period: 60 Days

Tools needed: Bracelet (supplied by me)

- If Helena catches herself complaining, she is to take the bracelet and move it to the other wrist. Because Helena is great in achieving goals, I knew she would stick with the time period. A shorter period of time may not offer the proper challenge.

- No gossiping - the same penalty applies.

- If Helena sees someone wearing the no-complaint bracelet and they start complaining and she points that fact out to them, she must switch her own no-complaint bracelet to the other wrist and start the 60 days over — because you've just complained about their complaining!

- Helena, pay attention to how you're speaking. If something happens that causes you discomfort, you are to simply make a statement of fact. If you keep going on and on about the issue, that's probably a complaint. Switch your bracelet to the other wrist and start over.

Follow-up:

Within 45 days, Helena reported she was more focused on the present moment. The value of her 'complaint jar' was decreasing. Helena also reported that she had been offered the "job" of her dreams.

Easy Action Steps to add a "No Pity Party Zone" to Your Spiritual Practice

- There are multiple solutions for every problem. Pick up a pencil and write down 7 possible solutions to the problem.
- Make a list of the "good" that is or has happened because of this problem.
- Ask for help and give yourself permission to accept it.

STOP HOSTING PITY PARTIES

Today is not only the first day of the rest of your life, it is a gift from the Universe stuffed full of memorable experiences and endless opportunities to choose your destiny.

Stephanie E. Wilson-Coleman, Ph.D.,
The Empowerment Doctor

STOP HOSTING PITY PARTIES

**PLAN
TO SUCCEED**

Prescription #5

"A goal without a plan is just a wish."

Antoine de Saint-Exupéry

Consultation with
PLAN TO SUCCEED

Seeker: I want to do something with my life.

Plan: Well, what do you want?

Seeker: I don't know, just something better than what I am doing.

Plan: Well, How do you feel?

Seeker: About what I want? I don't know HOW I feel.

Plan: What does that have to do with TODAY?

Seeker: Nothing I guess.

Plan: Well, when you know what you want, and how you feel about what you want, we can PLAN to be successful at WHATEVER YOU CHOOSE!

Diagnosis:
Fast Track Your Plan to Succeed

Many people talk about their desire to accomplish their dreams. Some want to write a book, go back to school or start a business, but they become overwhelmed when focusing on the end results and quickly blame their lack of success on "not knowing how" or "not receiving adequate support." Often not knowing how is reason enough for people to never get started. It is an indication that they do not really believe in their abilities. To succeed, one must first get started. Deep inside we know what to do, however, individuals fear giving up an established financial base that provides security for themselves and their families, so they abandon their soul desires and thus keep their dreams on hold.

In a 2008 follow up study, Self-Determination Theory: A Macro Theory of Human Motivation, Development, and Health, conducted by Edward L. Deci and Richard M. Ryan, at the University of Rochester, concluded that "intrinsic aspirations that include such life goals as affiliation, generativity and personal development . . . is associated with greater health, well-being and performance.'" Angelo Kinicki, organizational culture expert and W. P. Carey, School of Business professor (Arizona State University) says doing what you love will improve your mental health. "It is important to do something we love for a living because our work lives will then provide meaning and purpose, which are associated with psychological well-being and health."

The Merriam Webster dictionary defines aspirations as "a strong desire to achieve something great." However, in 2016, Stephanie Walden reported that a study, conducted by Trade Schools, College and University, an online career training resource, concluded that 78.6% of adults do not end up following through on the career path they dreamed of when they were six years old, but the 22% who did pursue their dream jobs were overwhelmingly happy with their careers, with 90% reporting high levels of job satisfaction.

Prescription:
It's all in your mindset

Dr. Kerry Schofield, Good & Company science team, reports on BrazenBlog.com, "The biggest roadblock between people and their dream job is their mindset." Merriam-Webster defines "mindset" as a fixed state of mind, a way of thinking: a person's attitude or set of opinions about something." Dr. Masters says, "Your mental atmosphere or state of mind is the key." In his book, *Awaken the Giant Within*, Tony Robbins says "most people treat a belief as if it's a thing, when really all it is, is a feeling of certainty about something. If you say you believe that you're intelligent, all you're really saying is I feel certain that I'm intelligent."

Barton Goldsmith, Ph.D., a psychotherapist and syndicated columnist, gives several reasons we don't chase our dreams. "You feel you don't deserve it; you feel that you don't have the time to take on anything more; you tell yourself that there's someone who is better than you." He advises, "Don't let yourself or anyone else talk you out of fulfilling your dreams."

How does one take the steps to improve their mental health? Begin by living an awakened life, a life with the highest vision of yourself. How is re-igniting dreams and awakening our souls accomplished? Begin with your **feelings**. Transforming our lives into our higher visions will awaken our souls. So why aren't the majority of us living our dreams?

Dosage:
Feelings - A Matter of the Heart

Jerry Savelle, president of Jerry Savelle Ministries International writes, "The greatest battles you will ever fight in your life are between your ears. Your mind is the battleground. Your mind is like a computer. It must be programmed. And it is being programmed with either negative thoughts, ideas and concepts or positive thoughts, ideas, and concepts every day of your life." Savelle continues, "According to this law of God in Galatians 6:7, *man determines his own happiness or misery based upon the seeds that he sows*. There are both positive seeds and negative seeds. You and I stand in a very strategic place where we are the only ones in our lives who possess the authority to determine which type of seeds we will sow. You have been given that authority. No one else can determine that for you."

Joshua Tilghman, the author of *The Spirit of the Scripture.com*, discusses Samson and Delilah, (Judges 16, **KJV**). "Samson represents our thoughts, our intellectual nature; Samson's hair is symbolic of our spiritual power; Delilah represents our feelings, emotions; and the Philistines represent thoughts that become our enemies; the temple represents our mind. Often, people allow emotions (feelings) to take over. Many react emotionally to a situation instead of making a conscious choice, and when ruled by emotions, some are blinded. When Samson destroyed the temple, he destroyed his negative thoughts." We are all Samson and the battle is between our ears.

Arnold M. Patent, author of *You Can Have It All*, says, "Emotions are feelings distorted by the thoughts that we have attached to the feelings. These beliefs are untrue but we created them to keep us away from our power so we can have human experiences." Patent created the Feeling Exercise to help remove labels from our feelings, so that we can increase our trust in ourselves and in others. Life is a feeling experience and we feel with our hearts.[2]

The Feeling Exercise by Arnold M. Patent (I really like this one)

Close your eyes and scan your body. Notice how you are feeling.

Feel the feeling free of any thoughts you have about it. Feel the energy, feel the power in the feeling.

1. Feel love for the feeling just the way it is. Feel love for the power in the feeling.
2. Feel love for yourself feeling the feeling and feeling the power in the feeling.

As you begin the process of feeling your feelings free of labels, notice the energy in the feeling and the intensity. Now feel the intensity of this energy as power, your own power. Patent reminds us that when we let go of judgments and open our hearts, we give ourselves the joy of feeling all the ways that we love ourselves and gain access to the aliveness, the wonder and the inspiration of life.

Life is a feeling experience and we feel through our hearts.

Meditation – the Next Step

Robert Gray Hawk Coke reminds us that using meditation can control complex emotions. "Our minds consist of the conscious mind which is approximately 12% of the mind and the subconscious mind which is approximately 88% of our mind. In order to change your mind and emotions, you have to work with the subconscious mind. We can tap into the subconscious mind through meditation."[3]

Gaiam.com recommends the following meditation technique for beginners.

> Sit or lie comfortably. You may even want to invest in a meditation chair.
>
> 1) Close your eyes.
> 2) Make no effort to control the breath; simply breathe naturally.
> 3) Focus your attention on the breath and on how the body moves with each inhalation and exhalation. Notice the movement of your body as you breathe. Observe your chest, shoulders, rib cage, and belly. Simply focus your attention on your breath without controlling its pace or intensity. If your mind wanders, return your focus back to your breath.

In the beginning, maintain this meditation practice for two to three minutes, then try it for longer periods.

Follow Up Appointment #1
Emotional Freedom Technique (EFT)[4]

In 1990, Dr. Roger Callahan developed a technique he named Thought Field Therapy (TFT), based upon traditional Chinese medicines and meridians. After numerous modifications, a set of simple sequence of points to tap were developed and proved to be effective no matter the situation. In 2014, Dawson Church, Ph.D. founded the National Institute of Integrative Healthcare to study and implement groundbreaking psychological and medical techniques. Dr. Church's team successfully proved that the EFT reduced stress levels of 83 subjects by 50 percent.

Below are EFT steps published by Tap into Heaven. I use this regularly.

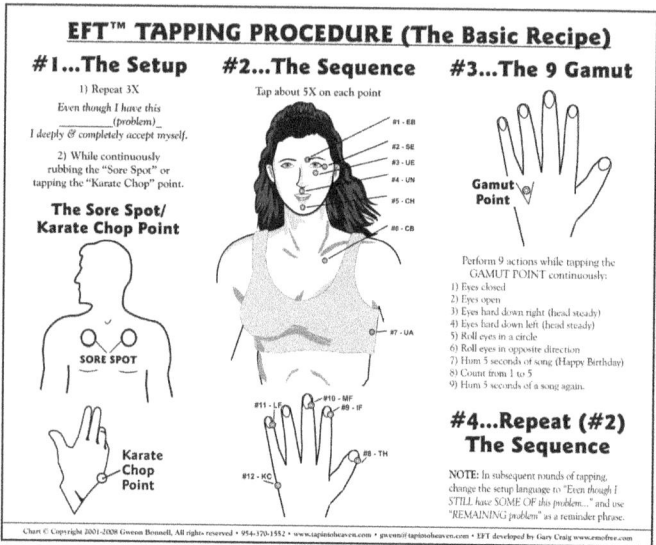

http://tapintoheaven.com/EFTshortcut/

Renewing of Your Mind

Ed and Deb Shapiro, personal development and meditation specialists, "believe that the role of the mind and emotions in our state of health is a vital one and that by understanding this relationship we can claim a greater role in our own well-being."

In Woody Allen's movie, **Manhattan**, Diane Keaton is breaking up with Allen's character and wants to know why he isn't angry. "I don't get angry," he replies. "I grow a tumor instead."

Romans 12:2 (ESV) says *"do not conform to this world, but be transformed by the renewal of the mind."* "Sometimes your heart needs more time to accept what your mind already knows," author anonymous.

The conscious mind can perform two of the most powerful functions. Mindset Habits.com lists these functions as:

1. The ability to direct your focus.
2. The ability to imagine that which is not real.

The subconscious mind takes orders from the conscious mind. So what you continuously focus on, the subconscious mind obediently delivers the feelings, emotions and memories that you have associated with these thoughts. This will keep you in an infinite loop.

Directing our thoughts is more powerful than we allow ourselves to believe. Unleashing your passion requires commitment and action. You cannot delegate it, wish it into existence or resurrect it with angel dust. It requires work and established goals.

Never limit yourself by believing that you do not have what it takes to achieve your goals because you do have what it takes. **You are the person you have been waiting for.**

Follow Up Appointment #2
Goal Setting – The Power of the Pen

After completing the Feeling Exercises, one can get ideas from the heart. These promptings will remain ideas until action is taken. *"Write the vision and make it plain on tablets, that he may run who reads it. For the vision is yet for an appointed time... But the just shall live by this faith."* Habakkuk 2:2-4 **(KJV)**

Goal Setting - The Success Experiment

An article in the *Huffington Post*:

For seven days, start your day by writing down your goals and dreams in the four key areas of life:

1. Health & relationships
2. Love & relationships
3. Vocation
4. Time & money freedom

Write down what you would truly **love**, no matter how big or bold it may seem to you right now.

This is a simple yet extremely powerful experiment and it will cause two things to happen. First, you will reach a new level of clarity of your goals and dreams. Secondly, your daily thought pattern focus will shift.

S.M.A.R.T. Goal Setting

A S.M.A.R.T. goal is a defined specific, measurable, actionable, results-focused and time-bound goal.

Specific Goal	How is the Goal Measured	Actions required to achieve the goal	Realistic and Reasonable Results	Timeline - When do you expect to complete the goal	Is it Enjoyable, Exciting and Ethical	Resources required

The benefits of setting S.M.A.R.T. goals according to Lean Blitz Consulting.com:

- Specific goals are monitored goals – this allows the conscious mind to give clear directions to the subconscious mind.
- Plans are incorporated - A good goal is a planned goal. A goal with specific details will necessitate planning how you'll go about achieving the goal.
- Progress is easy to monitor – You are able to determine what is working well and what needs to be modified. You are able to quickly identify missed targets and make adjustments easily.
- Easier to visualize how success will look.

"How do you eat an elephant? One bite at a time."
Creighton Abrams

Goals Require Action

The hardest part of achieving any success is healing the heart and a renewing of the mind. The rest is a by-product of a happy heart. Once goals are put into action, it is natural to expect to reach financial rewards. Renewing the mind also requires the change in habits and behaviors. Thomas J. Stanley, Ph.D., found that 80% to 86% of millionaires and deca-millionaires are self-made, and according to Entrepreneur.com, 62% of billionaires are self-made.

Beside setting and achieving goals, what are the behaviors?

Thomas Corley spent five years studying the daily activities of 233 rich people and 128 poor people. Corley's research identified more than 300 daily activities that separated the "haves" from "have-nots." The research study is detailed in his book, **Rich Habits.** Incorporating these habits into your lifestyle will put you on the path to creating an enhanced and prosperous life.[5]

Using the behaviors identified by Corley is an exercise that can help to identify which behaviors to change to increase your financial wealth.

YoProWealth detail the general beliefs that create several financial mindsets. Review the chart to identify your financial mindset. Once identified, determine the steps necessary to become financially independent.

Money Mindset: The Difference Between The Poor & The Rich

	Poor	Middle Class
Belief of Wealth	Matter of luck; be taken care of by 3rd party	Work hard & be self-sufficient
Money motto	Survival	Financial security
Mindset on Work	Don't do it	Do it yourself
Ways to Wealth	Play the lottery	Work hard, get as many credentials and be the 'smartest'
Financial Goal	Get a lucky break	Maximize income per hour
Career	Welfare	Corporate employee, doctor, realtor, etc.
# of Incomes	0-1	1
Level of Risk	No action, no risk	Risk averse
Get Paid Based On…	Need	Hours worked
Way to Get More Money	Ask for more help	Get a 2nd job
Extra Income Means…	All money is consumed	Expand spending
Success Means…	Don't have to work	Get credentials, be the smartest
Believe That They're…	Unlucky	Smart
Thoughts of the Rich	Disgust	Resentment
Education/Training Focus	None	Get as many credentials, be the 'smartest'
Plan For…	Right now	Next month

Which mentality do you have? Find out where you are weak, and then YoPro Wealth can help you make a plan to correct your mindset, and get you on the path towards financial freedom with the millionaire and even billionare mindset!

PLAN TO SUCCEED

So many people do not obtain financial freedom because they do not have one thing: **the right mindset.** Everything starts with how you think about money, wealth and success. Below are the general beliefs of the different wealth classes. Which mindset do you have? **YoPro Wealth: Take Control. Make Money. Live Wealthy.**

Millionaire	Billionaire
Be self-sufficient, but have multiple streams of income	Self-sufficient & must have multiple streams of income
Financial freedom	Freedom & make an impact
Outsource; have others do it	Build a team of smarter people than you to do it
Build systems & inspire your team	Build systems & inspire teams; leverage efforts of talented people
Maximize passive income (different industries)	Maximize passive income (within one industry)
Entrepreneurship, real estate rental, investing, online, etc.	Entrepreneurship; create a large business or movement
2+	2+
Calculated risks	Calculated, large, regular risks
Results	Results & impact
Add stream of income	Maximize or add a stream of income
Invest first, spend 2nd	Invest first, spend 2nd
Create freedom	Change the way the world works
Resourceful	Resourceful; not that "different" or smart
Admiration	Inspiration
Leading people	Understanding & leading people
5 Years out	20 Years out

For more information, visit YoProWealth.com

YoPro Wealth: Take Control. Make Money. Live Wealthy.

https://yoprowealth.com/wp-content/uploads/2013/12/Money-Class-Table.pdf

Platinum Money Rules — 10-10-10-70 Rule
Tithing — 10%

"For unto whomsoever much is given, of him shall be much required; and to whom men have committed much, of him they will ask the more."

Luke 12:48 (KJV)

Sir John Templeton, the mutual-fund pioneer, said, "I have observed 100,000 families over my years of investment counseling. I always saw greater prosperity and happiness among those families who tithed than among those who didn't."

John Rockefeller disclosed, "I would never have been able to tithe the first million dollars I ever made if I had not tithed my first salary, which was $1.50 per week."

The next are easy:
- 10 percent for retirement
- 10 percent for large purchases
- 70 percent for the remainder of your expenses

5. Golden Money Rules

Below are some well-known, often discussed Money Rules:
- Spend less than you make
- Have a plan
- Get out of debt
- Save and invest
- Take control of your financial life

Money is energy, and all energy is created with relationships to thoughts, feelings, images and action. How you feel about money plus how your money is circulated will determine your financial wealth. Developing a millionaire mind-set or consciousness is easy.

Since 86% of all millionaires and 62% of all billionaires are self-made, the odds of becoming a millionaire are better than the odds of winning the lottery.

Taking Action to Succeed
NOAH'S STORY

History:
Noah's major complaint is the inability to succeed further in his career. Noah feels as it nothing he does works and it always backfires.

Sessions:
During the first session, Noah spoke in detail about his frustrations. The major complaint with each scenario was the feeling of being held back. The more he talked, the angrier he became. I thought the "letter" exercise would be a great start.

Assignment:
Burning Bowl:
- List 3 things that you do not like about the people you believe are holding you back.
- Now scratch out their names and place your name in its place. Read the modified statements out loud and write down how you feel when you read the statements. Focus on the feelings only.
  - Describe a time before now that you have felt this way.
  - What are the recurring feelings?
- Write the feelings on a sheet of paper and burn it. As you watch the paper burn, know that these feelings are being transformed and released.

Write a Letter to Anger:
Recall an incident that has caused you pain. Write a letter to this anger saying exactly what you could not verbalize before.

Burn the letter.

Follow Up Appointment:

During the next follow up an appointment, Noah reported that he was feeling less and less that someone was holding him back. He now was ready to focus on what he could do to improve his life. I suggested that he use the letter technique weekly so that he can release the anger and heal his heart.

Next Assignment:
Visualization:

Visualizing Your Ideal Career:

- How do you define career success? Are you achieving some level of success in your current job? What job will help you achieve complete success?
- What would you want to do today if all your bills were paid and you had relatively unlimited cash reserves?
- What would your career be like if you had the power to make it any way you wanted?
- What would you like your obituary to say about your career accomplishments and the impact you left with the people you worked with?
- If absolutely no obstacles stood in the way of your achieving it, what would you most like to attain in your career?
- Who are the people you most admire? What is it about them or their careers that attract you to them? Is there something about what they have or do that you want for your career vision?
- Imagine yourself in the future at a point in which you have achieved great career success. What is it

that you have accomplished?
- What's the one activity you most love? Is it part of your career? If not, how can you make it part of your career?
- Where would you like to be in your career in 5 years? In 10 years? In 15 years?

Career Vision Statement:

Write a short vision statement along with a short description of how you currently see yourself accomplishing it - reaching your vision. Write everything in the present tense, as if you already have accomplished it. The mind does not know the difference between real or fantasy. This keeps your vision in the present.

Vision Board:

Once you've created your career vision statement, put it in places where you can see it. Read it often. Use pictures also to help you visualize.

Final Session:

During this session, Noah reported he was making success toward his dream job. He actually reported he had been offered an amazing job and was set to start in 2 weeks.

Noah asked if we could keep in touch regularly. I agreed.

Easy Action Steps to Help You Achieve Your Goals for Your Daily Spiritual Practice

- List seven reasons why you want this.
- Do 5 things a day toward this goal, no matter how small.
- Swap an hour of watching television for an hour of reading a book.

PLAN TO SUCCEED

In order to achieve success, you have to first awaken the millionaire that lives inside of you. Once the inner giant has awakened you will be able to jump-start the outer millionaire.

**Stephanie E. Wilson-Coleman, Ph.D.,
The Empowerment Doctor**

PLAN TO SUCCEED

GRATITUDE

Prescription #6

Be grateful for what you already have while you pursue your goals. If you aren't grateful for what you already have, what makes you think you would be happy with more.

Roy T. Bennett

Consultation with
GRATITUDE

Seeker: I guess I will be grateful when I get what I want.

Gratitude: Be grateful for what you have now.

Seeker: And what is that?

Gratitude: For having the life to even wonder what you have to be grateful for…

Seeker: Oh…

Diagnosis:
The Fuel Necessary to Live Your Dreams;
GRATITUDE

Love is the road to GRATITUDE. The word gratitude is derived from the Latin word "Gratia" which means "grace." Paul Pruyser, the author of *The Minister of Diagnostician*, further defines gratitude as "grace, graciousness or gratefulness, gifts, the beauty of giving and receiving or getting something for nothing."

> *"Give thanks in all circumstances."*
>
> **1 Thessalonians 5:18 (NIV)**

Everyone begins life with big dreams. It's not long before it is discovered that everything wanted in life comes with a price. There is no free lunch, no Easter bunny, no Santa Claus, no Knight in shining armor. Every life is filled with storms and celebrations, chaos and success, confusion and triumphs.

What does it take to be patient, knowing that everything has come to pass? No one is immune from the same challenges faced daily, not even the rich and famous.

> *"When you are climbing the mountains in your life, your success depends on whether you take things for granted or take them with gratitude."*
>
> **G.K. Chesterton**

When we are grateful, we become consciously aware of the many benefits, blessings, assistance, divine nudgings and grace we receive along our journey. No matter how confident you are or how well you think you are doing on your climb, there will be times when you start to believe that you can't make it; there will be times when the paper tigers of your life manage to slow you down; it is during these times that gratitude is most important. Remembering the blessings will serve as the fuel to keep you moving toward the fulfillment of your dreams.

Melody Beattie said, "Gratitude unlocks the fullness of life. It turns what we have into enough, and more. It turns denial into acceptance, chaos to order, and confusion to clarity. It can turn a meal into a feast, a house into a home, a stranger into a friend. Gratitude makes sense of our past, brings peace for today, and creates a vision for tomorrow."

Psychologists Robert Emmons and Michael McCullough found through their research that daily gratitude exercises resulted in increased enthusiasm, alertness, physical well-being, and energy. It was proven that gratitude expands flexible and creative thinking and aids in coping with stressful conditions. "To say we feel grateful is not saying that everything in our lives is necessarily great. It just means we are aware or our blessing."

In *Ask and It is Given*, Abraham-Hicks wrote, "Because the vibration of appreciation is the most powerful connection between the physical you and the non-physical you, this process will also put you in a position to receive even clearer guidance from your Inner Being. The more you practice appreciation, the less resistance you will have in your own vibrational frequencies. And the less resistance you have, the better your life will be."[1]

In a 2014 issue of The Today online column, David DeSteno wrote, "Thankfulness triggers patience and a willingness to hold out for greater monetary gain. On average, we increased people's financial patience by about 12 percent."

Dr. Masters says, "Gratitude is an acknowledgment in the mind that creates a positive state of mind that is self-perpetuating."

Prescription:
Steps to take

A popular way of acknowledging gratitude daily is to keep a journal. Gratitude journals range from plain notebooks to online programs. Journaling methods also vary. I have listed a few ways, but ultimately you must choose or design the method best for you.

Daily Journaling – Daily, write down a list of three (3) to ten (10) things for which you are grateful. This exercise can be completed in the morning or before going to bed at night. These simple exercises keep you focused on the good that is happening in your life. Often we forget the daily blessings we receive if we don't keep track of them.

> *"When you arise in the morning, give thanks for the morning light, for your life and strength. Give thanks for your food, and the joy of living. If you see no reason for giving thanks, the fault lies with yourself."*
>
> **Tecumseh, Shawnee Chief**

Gratitude Journal, the Dan Sullivan Method

Dan Sullivan, founder of The Strategic Coach and author of The Gratitude Principle says, "We can achieve endless progress and success in our lives as long as we are increasingly grateful each step along the way. Lack of gratitude is one of the biggest obstacles to personal progress."

Before you go to sleep tonight, take two minutes to answer these gratitude-inducing questions:

1. What am I grateful/thankful for?
2. Why am I thankful?
3. How can I express my gratitude?
4. First action to take?

Sullivan also recommends writing a gratitude letter to a person who has had a positive influence on you or who has helped you in ways that were beneficial.[1]

Rampage of Appreciation, Abraham-Hicks

Abraham-Hicks is well known for the Rampage of Appreciation Game included in the book *Ask and It Is Given*. The purpose of this game is to get the participant accustomed to the feeling of higher vibrations. The more you find something to appreciate, resistance to your "good" dissipates and your desire can easily flow into your experience. It can be played anyplace and anytime by simply directing pleasant thoughts in your mind. If you were to write your thoughts on paper it would enhance this process, but it is not absolutely necessary.

Here's how it works:

> Step 1 – Look around your immediate environment and try to notice something that is pleasing to you. Try to hold your attention on this pleasing object and ponder how wonderful, useful or beautiful it is. Your Positive Feeling will increase the longer you focus on it.

> Step 2 - Make it your intention to focus on objects that easily invoke your appreciation, this is not a process of finding something troubling and fixing it, this is a process of deliberately focusing your thoughts on the object to appreciate. The longer you hold on to these vibrations of appreciation, the more the law of attraction will bring you other thoughts, experiences, and people that match your current practiced vibration.[2]

Vibration of Appreciation is one of the highest forms of vibration. You will become used to it with practice.

> *"Whatever I am offered in devotion with a pure heart — a leaf, a flower, fruit or water — I accept with joy."*
>
> **Bhagavad Gita**

Dosage:
Comprehensive Journal

Because life's challenges are more extensive and often filled with teeth-rattling experiences, Harvard Health Publications recommends a gratitude process that combines popular items from some of the journals available on the market today.

Step 1 - Write a thank-you note. You can make yourself happier and nurture your relationship with another person by writing a thank-you note expressing your enjoyment and appreciation of that person's impact on your life. Send it, deliver it or read it in person, if possible. Make a habit of sending at least one gratitude note a month. Once in a while, write one to yourself.

Step 2 - No time to write? Thank someone mentally. It may help just to think about someone who has done something nice for you and mentally thank that individual.

Step 3 - Keep a gratitude journal. Make it a habit to write down, or share with a love one, your thoughts about the gifts you receive each day.

Step 4 - Count your blessings. Pick a time every week to sit down and write about your blessings, reflecting on what went right or what you are grateful for. Sometimes it helps to pick a number, such as three to five things, that you will identify each week. As you write, be specific and think about the sensations you felt when something good happened to you.

Step 5 - Pray. People who are spiritual can use prayer to cultivate gratitude.

Step 6 - Meditate. Mindfulness meditation involves focusing on the present moment without judgment. Although people often focus on a word or phrase, such as peace, it is also possible to focus on what you're grateful for (the warmth of the sun, a pleasant sound, etc.).

Follow Up Appointment #1

If you are concerned about how long or how often you should meditate, Do You Yoga suggests every day for approximately 5-10 minutes. You can start with 1 minute and add a minute daily until you reach the recommended length.

> *"You will be enriched in every way so that you can be generous on every occasion, and through us, your generosity will result in thanksgiving to God."*
>
> **2 Corinthians 9:11 (NIV)**

In today's supercharged world, the number of books filled with useful techniques to help us create a positive attitude is overwhelming. If tasked with choosing only one, choose one that promotes the colors of gratitude and appreciation. Using these colors are enough to guarantee one paints a pretty canvas. Staying focused on the good that is continually present in life requires us to always live in the present moment, in the now while turning a deaf ear to the tales of destruction that are forever seeking our attention. This magnificently opulent universe has flooded life with wonders. Become still enough every hour to appreciate these wonders.

Follow Up Appointment #2

Of course, when everything is going our way, appreciation and thanksgiving effortlessly roll off our tongues. It is when the blessings are wearing the colors of darkness, despair, envy and hatred that we become mute. It is during these times that we have to stay vigilant in keeping our attention on the good. We have to stay focused on the uplifting colors, because life is not one-dimensional. We can always find something to celebrate. There is always some reason to praise, to rejoice.

Each experience is filled with something marvelous. Use vision and focus to find it.

You create your life, so choose luscious colors. In all that you may experience, give praise, praise, praise.

In my book, *Is Anybody Listening,* I wrote, "Every day is a miracle, a gift from Infinite Kindness. If our vision is unclouded, we will see that the valleys are indeed wrapped in gold, filled with absolute wonder and loaded with consciousness-raising experiences."

GRATITUDE

"When you are grateful, you are focused on what is right in your life; and as you focus on what is right, you will begin to see the possibilities and not the obstacles. The veil will be removed from your eyes and you will be awakened to the abundance that surrounds you. If the only prayer you say in your life is "thank you," that would suffice."

Meister Eckhart

Ending the Struggle with Gratitude
WILLIAM'S STORY

History:

William complained that no matter what, he did not seem to find anything to be happy about. He said he always feels a little sad.

Sessions:

As we talked, William discussed a lot to be happy about, but he only concentrated on the major things. I thought it was time to amp up the gratitude.

Prescription:
Gratitude Journal:

For 30 days, William was to write down 3-5 things a day for which he was grateful. He was required to answer the following question daily — **What if you woke up today with only the things you were grateful for yesterday?**

Hug the Universe

William was assigned an exercise "Hug the Universe".

1. Stand outside so that you can see the sky.
2. Allow yourself a moment to feel centered and relaxed. Take a few slow, deep breaths in and out.
3. Now, stand with your arms outstretched to the sky. Feel connected to the vastness around you. Release any discomfort, uneasiness, and pain to the Universe. As you hold the intention, say out loud **"I now release my sadness, uneasiness, and pain to the Universe"**. Modify this statement for whatever comes up for you.
4. Imagine the emotions, thoughts, as being released to the sky. Picture it in whatever form you see - you

may see a shape, color, events, or people. See it being released from your body and floating to the Universe surrounded by white light.
5. Allow yourself to feel free.
6. Now allow the things you are grateful for to flood your mind. Feel yourself being made whole.

During the next session, William even looked happier and lighter. He said he never realized he had some much for which to be grateful.

Easy Steps to Help You add "Gratitude" to Your Spiritual Practice and Make it a Habit

I have discovered that when I really focus on what I have to grateful for this is easy, easy, easy.

- Write it down - daily make a list of 5 things you are grateful for. They don't have to be big things.
- Do you have shelter, food, internet, water, friends, electronics, family, even if you don't like them, shoes, clothes, nice weather, bad weather, another day alive, etc. You get the idea.
- Be grateful in advance – "I'm grateful for ____. (that things I want).
- List your talents, skills, etc.
- Things that you've done that you can brag about.

Listing 5 things a day, takes less than 5 minutes, but the benefits are amazing.

GRATITUDE

CONCLUSION
From Homeless to Hopeful

You read earlier that I was pregnant at 14, a mother at 15 and I graduated from high school in the top 7% of my class. Let's go a little further into my journey. By the time I was 18, I was anorexic, suicidal and had been sexually molested too many times to count. Any day that I did not consider suicide was a good day. At the age of 20, I graduated from college with two majors and a minor. I suffered a basal skull fracture, and to this day I do not have any sense of smell or taste. I married young and then divorced. Shortly after my divorce I experienced financial devastation and was reduced to homelessness. I was able to transcend these experiences and create abundance by seriously incorporating a few simple metaphysical principles into my daily life. I still have crazy days but I have learned how to flow through the craziness and not allow it to overtake me. I have also discovered that if you are not careful, your mind will convey untruths, so you have to be in constant control of your thoughts and change them when necessary.

Every time people see me, they want me to talk about money, especially how to accumulate money. Regardless of where you find yourself, the magic of this moment is that this is your only point of power. In this moment, you can do all of the things you need to do, because the Divine Mind is equally present right here. The power of the universe is available to you right here, right now, at this moment. We have to move away from the idea that the Divine Mind is working miracles, just not in our lives.

I remember hearing Rev. Michael Beckwith say in one of his lesson sermons "all of the universe that we need is present right here." I believe that the Divine Mind is working miracles in everyone's life; however, there are certain tools that you have to use. You have to step away from the problems/troubles and step away from trying "to work the law" and start to focus on the steps you need to take to actually get the universal laws to work for you. There are certain tools we have access to all the time. Regardless of whether you are rich or poor, short or tall, fat or skinny, sick or well; you have access to all the universal laws, which contains all the tools that you need to jumpstart your life.

I believe that every moment is filled with all the possibilities life has to offer. One can find happiness, sorrow, joy and sadness. One can find prosperity, poverty, abundance and lack. *"It is said that life is a canvas and we color it with acts of beauty, kindness, generosity and self-expression,"* author anonymous. The question we must answer is, "what acts are we using to color our prosperity?"

Often people feel that talking about money, abundance or prosperity is contradictory to the devout religious way of living. *"Be ye transformed by the renewing of your mind,"* Romans 12:2 (KJV) This well known bible verse reminds us that we are and should always be renewing our minds; but are we changing the way we think and feel about money? As I allowed myself to embrace various universal laws, I was able to transform my poverty.

Money is energy, and all energy is creating with our relationship and with our thoughts, feelings, images and actions. How you feel about money plus how you circulate money will determine your financial wealth. To "Be a Millionaire" you must develop a millionaire mindset or consciousness. So, I recommend dumping the **lottery consciousness** and replace it with the **abundance consciousness** and get ready to live your success.

Moment to moment we decide if we are coloring our lives and our experiences with prosperity or poverty. We all have access to the same power. Until we learn to better control our thoughts and stay in alignment with the will of the Divine Mind, we will always create a life filled with a smorgasbord of experiences. In spite of the circumstances, we still have a choice. Choose these easy practices of Forgiveness, Gratitude, Visualization, Staying in the Moment, Stop Hosting Pity Parties and Planning to Succeed to stay in the alignment with the Divine. These practices help you to continually focus on the good that is always present in your life.

It seems that weekly we are in awe of what quantum physicists discover. We now know that everything in our universal plane is interconnected and made up of energy. Scientists also agree that we have the undeniable ability to choose how we will respond to the drama in our lives. Our actions operate as some sort of a conductor to attract items with the same frequency, vibration, to us. So how do we harness this readily available mechanism? The use of visualization, creative or otherwise, is the answer. Sustained visualization will soften your resistance and increase your vibration toward your dream. Once you can hold this positive

CONCLUSION

vibration use your vision. You create your own life, so choose pretty colors.

Staying in the moment is essential. We cannot travel back in time and change it. We do not have the power to change what someone said, what we did or what we would have done. Our only point of power is in this moment. Stay in this moment! When we start to think about what someone said or did we make it real and relive that moment. When we do this, we are actually spending valuable time reliving something that has already happened and robbing ourselves of the value in the present moment.

My life now is a testament to refusing to dwell on the negative by hosting pity parties. My life has been filled with hard-hat experiences. To alter my emotions regarding some of the events in my life, I needed to think better thoughts, and I was able to achieve that by consciously deciding to remember only the good from my experiences. The more you practice this technique, the easier it becomes. Any improvement in your feeling nature, your emotional state will truly be your sip of inspiration. In all that you may experience, give praise, praise, and more praise.

After you create your success, you must learn the principles of money. The basic principle of money is 10% for tithing, 10% for retirement, and 10% for savings and 70% for your expenses. Rev. Evelyn Boyd, at Christ Universal Temple in Chicago, defines tithing as the rent you pay for living in this universe. You tithe where you are spiritually fed. According to Moneywise5.com, the Rockefeller's were taught to tithe 10% to a charitable cause; 10% to savings and account for every penny. I have learned that if you do not tithe, the universe will get its money in the form of accidents, illnesses or unplanned instances. If you add up the money you spend on unplanned instances or accidents it will equal 10% of your income. It would have been much easier to tithe. The discipline in the action is key.

Moving from a story of fear to a story of love requires you to sift through your thoughts and alter the negative thoughts to positive thoughts. You must answer the question, "what would I do if I knew I would not fail?" Next create a plan to make your answer, your vision a reality. Then when you and others look back at your life story, the chapters will be filled with triumph, victory, celebrations, abundance, and love.

Now is the time to start to paint a pretty canvas and create a life where you are the winner.

CREATING A MASTERPIECE FROM A MASTER MESS

"Every day is a miracle, a gift from Infinite Kindness. If our vision is unclouded, we will see that the valleys are indeed wrapped in gold, filled with absolute wonder and loaded with consciousness-raising experiences."

**Stephanie E. Wilson-Coleman, Ph.D.,
The Empowerment Doctor**

_____
_____
_____
_____
_____
_____
_____
_____
_____
_____
_____
_____
_____
_____

CONCLUSION

EPILOGUE

Throughout our lives, we will experience successes and breakthroughs. We will also experience disappointments, challenges and setbacks. Because society uses our failures to determine the value of our lives, we often allow ourselves to become immersed in our failures, making it difficult to move past them. It is at this point that you must remember that failure is not fatal or final and if handled properly what you learn from failure can become the ladder to your success.

When we are living the story of failure we are allowing what we think we believe to determine our success. Proceed with caution when depending solely on your thoughts. We have all allowed an assortment of characters to take up residence in our minds. If you actually take a little time to acknowledge your thoughts, you will find that you think thoughts that you do not believe or believe things that are not true and many of us do not know the difference. Taking steps daily to purify your thoughts is paramount.

Arnold M. Patent, the author of *The Journey*, says, "the feeling of inner conflict is one of the strategies we employ to keep the **power** hidden and we have all created the illusion of conflict."

Our lives are examples of the stories we are currently living; examples of the strategies we used to create lack and limitation. Are you living a story of love, a life filled with peace, joy, harmony, laughter and prosperity? Or are you living a story of fear, a life filled with envy, jealousy, persecution, lies, and lack?

As I began to practice the principles discussed in Catherine Ponder's book, I learned that gratitude, visualization, staying in the moment and transforming my tendency to focus on the negative began to change my life in ways that seemed magical. These techniques have helped me to stay focused on the goodness of the hidden power within by showing me how to create more goodness while **downsizing** room for conflict. I discovered the missing elements. The more I integrated metaphysical spiritual principles into my life, the faster things changed for the better. I was amazed at what I could accomplish a short period of time.

As we continue to explore spiritual principles on abundance, it is necessary to reiterate the formula for success in every area of our lives which includes **Forgiveness** – refusing to re-live the pain of the past in your future; **Gratitude** – focusing on what you have to be grateful for will improve your health and set-up a vibration that will draw more exciting things into your life; **Visualization** – as you create a mind movie that focuses on your success, you will automatically decrease the time you spend repeating negative situations; **Staying in the Moment** – eliminates multi-tasking and allows you to master what you are engaged in, in that moment; **Stop Hosting Pity Parties** – I discovered that what you focus on is what you create; **Plan to Succeed** – reminded me that failing to plan is planning to fail.

The more I used these techniques, these principles, the more happiness, and prosperity I was able to experience as well as establish a better connection with the Divine, God.

The universal power that is within us is always knocking. If we answer the knock, we can eliminate any lack or limitation in our lives and can start and continue on the journey to wholeness and **ignite our inner millionaire**.

RESOURCES

WORKSHEETS TO SUCCESS
Financial Healing Prescription

Part I – Make an Audio Recording
1. Using your favorite affirmations
2. Length approximately 5 minutes
3. Use soothing 'new age' music as the background
4. Sample Affirmations should also include intend statements
   - I am a magnet for money. Prosperity of every kind is drawn to me.
   - I think big, and then I allow myself to accept even more good from life.
   - I have unlimited choices. Opportunities are everywhere.
   - Life supplies all y needs in great abundance. I trust life.
   - I move from poverty thinking to prosperity thinking, and my finances reflect this change.

Part II – Meditation/Visualization
1. Twice a day – immediately upon rising and prior to going to sleep
2. Concentrate on your breaths; taking 4-5 seconds to inhale and exhale
3. Repeat to yourself a mantra you like; I simply repeat the word "God"
4. During this meditation, visualize yourself having, doing, or being that you wish to have, do or be

5. Visualize writing the checks to pay all the bills, living in your new home, etc
6. After each visualization, give thanks for its' manifestation

Part III – Power of the Spoken Word
1. Now is the time to heal yourself. Refrain from the desire to heal or help others
2. Only talk about the things you wish to appear in your life, i.e., instead of verbalizing negative things, talk only about the good things. Refuse to contribute to "negative" conversations

Part IV – Gratitude Journal
1. Maintain a written record of your blessings. Daily, list five (5) things that happened to you that you are grateful for.

Part V – Create a Vacuum
1. Discard or donate anything you have not used in approximately 12 months

BLUEPRINT TO FINANCIAL SUCCESS
PART ONE

How Did You Get Here?

Childhood Memories

In order to create financial wealth, you have to identify "how did you get where you are financially". Most financially behaviors are learned as children. We often "inherit" our parents' behavior around money.

Some common behaviors are: 1) parents never talked about money; parents lived miserly; 3) parents over spent; parents never invested; parents separated and/or divorced.

Exercise:
List two early childhood memories surrounding money. Give each example a "Title."

_____

_____

_____

_____

_____

_____

_____

_____

_____

RESOURCES

RESOURCES

What behaviors did you learn?

_____

_____

_____

_____

_____

_____

_____

Is the memory accurate?

_____

_____

_____

_____

_____

_____

_____

RESOURCES

How would others who were involved in this event remember the event?

_____

_____

_____

_____

_____

_____

_____

What behaviors did you adopt as a result of this?

_____

_____

_____

_____

_____

_____

TAPPING FOR SHIFTING YOUR PARADIGM
PART TWO

Your Savings and Trauma

Financial Trauma

Trauma comes from an event that shocks you and creates great distress or suffering, both during the event and after it's over.

Regardless of how long ago the event occurred, its negative effect could still be seen in your emotions and finances.

Exercise:
Write down the amount in your savings right now. If you have none and/or have debt, just put the number $0. Just below this number, write down how much you'd love to have in your savings account.

_____

_____

_____

_____

_____

_____

_____

_____

_____

RESOURCES

A. Amount in Savings Now

_____

_____

_____

_____

_____

_____

_____

B. Amount you would like to have

_____

_____

_____

_____

_____

_____

_____

RESOURCES

Now, say out aloud "It's not enough".
How does that statement make you feel?

___

Look at your savings again, think about any related past events that still linger in your thoughts in a negative way, and ask, "What does this mean about me? Write what you are feeling below.

___

Now look at the amount in your savings account and the gap between that and the amount you would like to have, and fill in the blank: This means I'm _____?

How would others who were involved in this event remember the event?

RESOURCES

What behaviors did you adopt as a result of this?

_____

_____

_____

_____

_____

_____

_____

_____

TAPPING SCRIPT FOR A FINANCIAL TRAUMA
PART THREE

Shifting from Impossible to Possible

The Outrageously Big Goal

Set a short term goal and an outrageously big goal that is outside of your current earnings.

Short Term Goal:

_____

_____

_____

_____

_____

_____

Outrageously Big Goal:

_____

_____

_____

RESOURCES

_____

_____

_____

_____

_____

Exercise:

Imagine yourself earning at the "outrageously big goal" in your future.

When I am earning that much, I finally feel:

_____

_____

_____

_____

_____

_____

_____

_____

I'll finally know that I am:

_____

_____

_____

_____

_____

_____

_____

I will have finally proved that I am:
(Proved what and/or to whom)?

_____

_____

_____

_____

_____

_____

_____

RESOURCES

List below at least 5 reason "WHY" you want this goal.

1.

2.

3.

4.

RESOURCES

5.

RESOURCES

You may consider adding EFT Tapping to increase effectiveness. (Emotional Freedom Techniques)

PERSONAL SWOT ANALYSIS WORKSHEET

The SWOT analysis is commonly used in business; however, you can use this worksheet to do your own personal SWOT analysis. The results will help you to identify your strengths and manage your weaknesses in order maximize your opportunities.

STRENGTHS:
- What activities do you do well/excel at?
- What relevant knowledge, experience or natural capability do you bring to your role?
- What are your personality strengths?
- What activities do you have a passion for?
- What do others see as your strengths?
- Which strengths are required for success in your role?

WEAKNESSES:
- What could you improve?
- What are your limitations?
- Which activities are in conflict with your natural style?
- What are others likely to see as weaknesses?
- What tasks or responsibilities do you dread?
- Where do you feel over committed?

OPPORTUNITIES:
- How can you turn your strengths into opportunities?
- What knowledge or experience could you gain to address current weaknesses?
- What resources do you have available to you to increase your capacity to act?
- How can your peers help you?

THREATS:
- What trends could harm you?
- What threats do your weaknesses expose you to?
- What obstacles are in your life?

CREATING A MASTER PIECE FROM A MASTER MESS

Notes

Forgiveness
Works Cited:

1. Ray, Sondra. *Loving Relationships.* Web http://firmsfoodcom/9919.html.

2. Wilson-Coleman, Stephanie. *Is Anybody Listening? A Journey to Wholeness.* The Champagne Connection, 2001, Print.

3. Sagan, Carl. *Pale Blue Dot: A Vision of the Human Future in Space,* Ballantine Books. 1997 Edition, Print.

4. Byrne, Rhonda. *The Secret.* Atria Books, 2006, Print.

5. Baylor University. *The Values of Beliefs of the American Public.* September 2011.

6. Polizane. Wealth Inequality in America, YouTube, May 2013

7. Bureau of Labor Statistics, The Employment Situation – August 2016, USDL-16-1771

8. Hirsch, Todd. *This extended interview is a web exclusive from Type A. An edited version of this interview aired on CBC Radio One Monday, March 12, 2012, at 2:00 p.m. and Friday, March 16, 2012, at 8:00 p.m. (half an hour later in Newfoundland and parts of Labrador)*

9. Peace Pilgrim. Web. www.proverbsway.com

10. Tipping, Colin. *Radical Forgiveness.* Gateway, 2000

11. Corley, Thomas C. *Rich Habits.* Landon Street Press, 2009, Print.

12. Robinson JP & Martin S (2008). What do happy people do? Social Indicators Research; DOI 10.1007/s11205-008-9296-6.

13. Hill, Napoleon. *Think & Grow Rich.* Fall River Press, 2012 Edition, Print.

14. Lanphear, Roger. *Wealth Consciousness: A Guide from Babaji for Prosperity.* Author's Choice Press, 2000, Print.

15. Myss, Carolyn. *Entering the Castle: Finding the Inner Path to God and Your Soul's Purpose.* Free Press: A Division of Simon & Schuster, Inc., 2007, Print

16. Lipton, Bruce. *The Biology of Belief.* Mountain of Love Productions, 2005 https://www.bigquestionsonline.com/2014/08/04/what-does-quantum-physics-have-with-you/

17. Loyd, Alexander. *The Love Code: The Secret Principle to Achieving Success in Life, Love, and Happiness.* Harmony Books, 2015, Kindle eBook

Other Works Cited:

Cohen, Lorraine. "9 Ways Un-forgiveness Blocks Wealth, Health and Happiness." Web, Lorraine Cohen. www.lorrainecohen.com

Unity School of Christianity. *Metaphysical Bible Dictionary.* 1958, Print.

Gallup. Americans' Financial Worries Edge Up in 2016. 2016, Print

Foundation for Inner Peace. *A Course in Miracles, Volume Two, Workbook for Students.* Coleman Graphics, Eight Printing, December 1980, Print

Foundation for Inner Peace. *A Course in Miracles, Workbook for Student.* Coleman Graphics, Eight Printing, December 1980, Print

The PEW Forum on Religion and Public Life. *U.S. Religious Landscape Survey.* Pew Forum Web Publishing and Communications, February 2008.

NOTES

The Holy Bible: King James Version, Web

The Holy Bible: New International Version, Web

The Nielsen Total Audience Report, Q2 2016

Masters, Paul Leon. *Master's Degree Curriculum.* 2 vols. Burbank, CA: Burbank Printing, 2012. Print.

-- Ministers/Bachelor Curriculum. 4 Vols. Burbank, CA: Burbank Printing, 2012. PDF File.

Visualization:
Works Cited:

1. Butterworth, Eric. *Spiritual Economics.* Unity House, 2001, Print

2. "Successful People who use the Power of Visualization". MindBodyGreen.com. http://www.mindbodygreen.com/0-20630/8-successful-people-who-use-the-power-of-visualization.html. Web 31 Jan. 2017

3. Goddard, Neville, *Awakened Imagination*, n.p., PDF

4. "Aphantasia. (http://aphant.asia/faq?catid=0&faqid=1). Web 2 Feb 2017
   "What is Aphantsia?" Web http://aphant.asia/

5. Berkin, Alexandra. *"Visualization means working with the Imagination."* https://studybuddhism.com/en/advanced-studies/vajrayana/tantra-theory/visualization-practice-in-tantra. Web, 2 Feb. 2017

6. "If You Can't Imagine, How Can You Learn?". https://www.theguardian.com/education/2016/jun/04/aphantasia-no-visual-imagination-impact-learning. Web 2 Feb 2017

7. Dobrowolski, Patti. Drawing Soltins, Creative Genius Press, 2011, Print

8. https://positivepsychologyprogram.com/mindfulness-exercises-techniques-activities/

Other Works Cited:

Center of American Progress, "Basic Statistics". https://talkpoverty.org, n.p. 2 Feb 2017

"Be What You Wish; Be What You Believe." Radio Talk, Station KECA, July 1951, Los Angeles. http://realneville.com/txt/radio_lectures.htm. Web. 30 Jan. 2017

Bon, Robert and Hallowell, Edward. http://www.tech21century.com/the-human-brain-is-loaded-daily-with-34-gb-of-information/

Brain Rules. www.brainrules.net/vision. Web. 2 Feb 2017

Gawain, Shakti. *Creative Visualization.* Nataraj Publishing, 1978, Print

Isaac, A. R. (1992). Mental Practice- Does it Work in the Field? The Sport Psychologist, 6, 192-198. Healthpsych.Psy.Vanderbuild.edu/HealthPsych/mentalimagery.html. Web. 30 Jan 2017.

Jeannerod, M. (1994). Mental Imagery in the Motor Context. http://citeseerx.ist.psu.edu/viewdoc/download?doi=10.1.1.120.6640&rep=rep1&type=pdf. Web, 31 Jan. 2017.

Staying in the Moment:
Works Cited:

1. Nolen-Hoeksema, S., Wisco, B., Lyuboirsky, S. (1991). Rethinking Rumination. Perspectives on Psychological Science.
2. Kabat-Zinn, Jon. (1979). An Outpatient Program in Behavioral

Medicine for Chronic Pain Patients Based on the Practices of Mindfulness Meditation: Theoretical Considerations and Preliminary Results.

3. Gregoire, S., Bouffard, T., Vezeau, C. (2012). Personal goal setting as mediator of the relationship between mindfulness and wellbeing. International Journal of Wellbeing, 2(3), 236-250. Doi:10.5502/ijw.v2.i3.5

4. https://positivepsychologyprogram.com/mindfulness-exercises-techniques-activities/

5. 'By Imagination Be Welcome." Radio Talk, Station KECA, July 1951, Los Angeles. http://realneville.com/txt/radio_lectures.htm. Web. 30 Jan. 2017

Other Works Cited:

Robbins, Tony. Awaken the Giant Within: How to Take Immediate Control of Your Mental, Emotional and Physical and Financial Destiny. Free Press, 1991, Print.

Most People have Unwanted, Worrying thoughts – Live Science. http://www.livescience.com/44687-most-people-have-unwanted-thoughts.html. Web 16 Mar 2017Stop Hosting Pity Parties

Eckart Tolle Describes Two Simple Exercises to Help You Live In The Now (VIDEO)

http://www.huffingtonpost.com/2014/03/25/eckhart-tolle-a-new-earth-exercises-present-now_n_5024829.html

22 Mindfulness Exercises, Techniques & Activities for Adults (+PDF's)

https://positivepsychologyprogram.com/mindfulness-exercises-techniques-activities/ 20 Mar 2017

Wallace, B. Alan. Minding Closely, The Four Applications of Mindfulness.

Snow Lion Publication. 2011, PDF

Whipple, M., Lewis, T., Sutton-Tyrell, K., Matthews, K. Barinas-Mitchell, E. Powell, L., Everson-Rose, S. Hopelessness, Depressive Symptoms, and Carotid Atherosclerosis in Women. 2009 Oct;40(10):3166-72. doi: 10.1161/STROKEAHA.109.554519. Epub 2009 Aug 27.

Pruyser, Paul. The Minister as Diagnostician: Personal Problems in Pastoral Perspective. Westminster Press, 1976, Print

Stop Hosting Pity Parties
Works Cited:
1. Dale Carnegie quote: http://thinkpositive30.com/blog/2014/09/02/feeling/

Other Works Cited:
Savelle, Jerry. The Battle between Your Ears. Web. http://www.cfaith.com/index.php/blog/36-articles/christmas/15653-the-battle-is-between-your-ears. Web 31 Jan. 2017

Self-Pity: 11 Tell-Tale Signs That You're Self-Inflicted Victim. https://lonerwolf.com/self-pity/. Web 3 Mar 2017

Why Ruminating is Unhealthy and How to Stop https://psychcentral.com/blog/archives/2011/01/20/why-ruminating-is-unhealthy-and-how-to-stop/. Web. 12 Mar 2017

Plan to Succeed
Other Works Cited:
1. Deci, E. and Ryan, R. Self-Determination Theory: A Macrotheory of Human Motivation, Development, and Health. 2008. Canadian Psychology, 200, Vo. 49, No. 3, 182-185
2. Patent, Arnold, M. *You Can Have It All: A Simple Guide to a Joyful*

and Abundant Life. Good Times Books Pvt. Ltd/Celebration Publishing, 2013, Print.

3. Coke, Robert Gray Hawk, https://www.manataka.org/page1149.html. Web.

4. Church, Dawson, Ph.D., Clinical EFT as an Evidence-Based Practice for the Treatment of Psychological and Physiological Conditions. Psychology, 2013. Vol4, No. 8 645-654

5. Corly, Thomas C. *Rich Habits.* Langdon Street Press, 2009, Print

Other Works Cited:

The Journey. Celebration Publishing, 2010, Print.

Matthews, Gail. Goal Research Summary. http://www.dominican.edu/academics/ahss/undergraduate-programs/psych/faculty/assets-gail-matthews/researchsummary2.pdf. Web, 1 Mar 2017

Goal Setting Research. http://happierhuman.com/goal-setting-research/

Burley. John. Money Secrets of the Rich. Morgan James Publishing, LLC. 2010. Print

Business News Daily. http://www.businessnewsdaily.com/7995-reasons-to-do-what-you-love.html

Byrne, Rhonda. The Secret. Atria Books, 2006, Print

Deschene, Lori. http://tinybuddha.com/blog/4-myths-about-doing-what-you-love-for-work/. Web. 15 Mar 2017

Steno, David (2014). Gratitude: A Tool for Reducing Economic Impatience. Psychological Science 2014, Vol 25(6) 1262-1267).

NOTES

Gratitude
Works Cited:

1. Sullivan, Dan. *The Gratitude Principle.* The Strategic Coach, 1996-2006, Print

2. Hicks, Jerry and Ester. Ask and It is Given. Hay House, Inc. 2004, Print

Other Works Cited:

Loveland-Coen, Victoria. The Gratitude Experiment, www.gratitudexp.com/tag/michael¬beckwith/

Vitale, Joe. Zero Limits Answers. Hypnotic Marketing, Inc., 2009

The Holy Bible: Holman Christian Standard Bible. Web.

Brown, Michael. *Finding the Field.* www.findingthefield.com

Emmons, R.A. & McCullough, M.E. (2003). Counting Blessings Versus Burdens: An Experimental Investigation of Gratitude and Subjective Well-Being in Daily Life. *Journal of Personality and Social Psychology*, Vol 84, No. 377-389

Foundation for Inner Peace. *A Course in Miracles*, Volume One Text. Coleman Graphics, Eight Printing, December 1984, Print

The Holy Bible: New International Version, Web

Holy Bible: King James Version, Web

Holy Bible: New International Version, Web

Masters, Paul Leon. *Master's Degree Curriculum*. 2 vols. Burbank, CA: Burbank Printing, 2012. Print.

--- Ministers/Bachelor Curriculum. 4 Vols. Burbank, CA: Burbank Printing, 2012. PDF File.

NOTES

Merriam-Webster Dictionary, Web

"Physics and Consciousness, Quantum Interconnectedness, Nature of Mind, Body and Spirit." Starstuffs.com/physcon/science.html. Web, 30 Jan. 2017

"The Third Universal Truth: Everything is Connected." FindingtheField.com. Web, 30 Jan. 2017

Tolle, Eckert. *The Power of Now*. Namaste Publishing, 1999. PDF

US San Diego News Center http://ucsdnews.ucsd.edu/pressrelease/u.s._media_consumption_to_rise_to_15.5_hours_a_day_per_person_by_2015. Web 19 Mar 2017

Wilson-Coleman, *Is Anybody Listening: A Journey to Wholeness*. Champagne Connection, 2001, Print.

--- *Embracing Life's Lessons*. The Champagne Connection. 2004, Print
--- *Be Sure You Dance: Life's Lessons to help you make every moment count*. The Champagne Connection. 2010, Print

APPENDIX

Following are references, books, research and scholars, used and quoted in this publication.

Ray, Sondra. *Loving Relationships*. Web http://firmsfoodcom/9919.html.

Wilson-Coleman, Stephanie. *Is Anybody Listening? A Journey to Wholeness*. The Champagne Connection, 2001, Print.

Sagan, Carl. *Pale Blue Dot: A Vision of the Human Future in Space*, Ballantine Books. 1997 Edition, Print.

Byrne, Rhonda. *The Secret*. Atria Books, 2006, Print.

Unity School of Christianity. *Metaphysical Bible Dictionary*. 1958, Print.

Baylor University. *The Values of Beliefs of the American Public*. September 2011. Polizane. Wealth Inequality in America, YouTube, May 2013

Gallup. Americans' Financial Worries Edge Up in 2016. 2016, Print

Bureau of Labor Statistics, The Employment Situation – August 2016, USDL-16-1771

Foundation for Inner Peace. *A Course in Miracles*, Volume Two, Workbook for Students. Coleman Graphics, Eight Printing, December 1980, Print

Foundation for Inner Peace. *A Course in Miracles, Workbook for Student*. Coleman Graphics, Eight Printing, December 1980, Print

Peace Pilgrim. Web. www.proverbsway.com

Hirsch, Todd. *This extended interview is a web exclusive from* Type A. *An edited version of this interview airs on CBC Radio One Monday, March 12, 2012, at 2:00 p.m. and Friday, March 16, 2012, at 8:00 p.m. (half an hour later in Newfoundland and parts of Labrador)*

Tipping, Colin. *Radical Forgiveness*. Gateway, 2000

APPENDIX

The PEW Forum on Religion and Public Life. U.S. Religious Landscape Survey. Pew Forum Web Publishing and Communications, February 2008.

The Holy Bible: King James Version, Web

The Holy Bible: New International Version, Web

Corley, Thomas C. *Rich Habits*. Landon Street Press, 2009, Print.

Robinson JP & Martin S (2008). What do happy people do? Social Indicators Research; DOI 10.1007/s11205-008-9296-6.

The Nielsen Total Audience Report, Q2 2016

Masters, Paul Leon. *Master's Degree Curriculum.* 2 vols. Burbank, CA: Burbank Printing, 2012. Print.

-- Ministers/Bachelor Curriculum. 4 Vols. Burbank, CA: Burbank Printing, 2012. PDF File.

Hill, Napoleon. *Think & Grow Rich*. Fall River Press, 2012 Edition, Print.

Lanphear, Roger. *Wealth Consciousness: A Guide from Babaji for Prosperity*. Author's Choice Press, 2000, Print.

Myss, Carolyn. *Entering the Castle: Finding the Inner Path to God and Your Soul's Purpose*. Free Press: A Division of Simon & Schuster, Inc., 2007, Print

Loveland-Coen, Victoria. The Gratitude Experiment, www.gratitudexp.com/tag/michaelbeckwith/

Vitale, Joe. *Zero Limits Answers*. Hypnotic Marketing, Inc., 2009 The Holy Bible: Holman Christian Standard Bible. Web.

Lipton, Bruce. The Biology of Belief. Mountain of Love Productions, 2005 https://www.bigquestionsonline.com/2014/08/04/what-does-quantum-physics-have-with-you/

APPENDIX

Loyd, Alexander. *The Love Code: The Secret Principle to Achieving Success in Life, Love, and Happiness.* Harmony Books, 2015, Kindle eBook

Cohen, Lorraine. "9 Ways Un-forgiveness Blocks Wealth, Health and Happiness." Web, Lorraine Cohen. www.lorrainecohen.com

"Peace Pilgrim." Proverbsway.com. Proverbsway, n.d. Web. 2 Dec. 2016

"Radical Forgiveness Summary Review." Soundstrue.com. Soundstrue, n.d. Web. 2 Dec. 2016

"Aphantasia. (http://aphant.asia/faq?catid=0&faqid=1). Web 2 Feb 2017 "What is Aphantsia?" Web http://aphant.asia/

"Be What You Wish; Be What You Believe." Radio Talk, Station KECA, July 1951, Los Angeles. http://realneville.com/txt/radio_lectures.htm. Web. 30 Jan. 2017

Berzin, Alexandra. "Visualization means working with the Imagination." https://studybuddhism.com/en/advanced-studies/vajrayana/tantra-theory/visualization-practice-in-tantra. Web, 2 Feb. 2017

Bon, Roger and Hallowell, Edward. http://www.tech21century.com/the-human-brain-is-loaded-daily-with-34-gb-of-information/

Brain Rules. www.brainrules.net/vision. Web. 2 Feb 2017

Brown, Michael. Finding the Field. www.findingthefield.com

Burley. John. Money Secrets of the Rich. Morgan James Publishing, LLC. 2010. Print

Business News Daily. http://www.businessnewsdaily.com/7995-reasons-to-do-what-you-love.html

Butterworth, Eric. *Spiritual Economics.* Unity House, 2001, Print

APPENDIX

"By Imagination Be Welcome." Radio Talk, Station KECA, July 1951, Los Angeles. http://realneville.com/txt/radio_lectures.htm. Web. 30 Jan. 2017

Byrne, Rhonda. *The Secret*. Atria Books, 2006, Print
Center of American Progress, "Basic Statistics". https://talkpoverty.org, n.p. 2 Feb 2017 Church, Dawson, Ph.D., Clinical EFT as an Evidence-Based Practice for the Treatment of Psychological and Physiological Conditions. Psychology, 2013. Vol4, No. 8 645-654

Coke, Robert Gray Hawk, https://www.manataka.org/page1149.html. Web.

Corley, Thomas C. Rich Habits. Langdon Street Press, 2009, Print Carnegie, Dale quote: http://thinkpositive30.com/blog/2014/09/02/feeling/

Deci, E. and Ryan, R. Self-Determination Theory: A Macrotheory of Human Motivation, Development, and Health. 2008. Canadian Psychology, 200, Vo. 49, No. 3, 182-185

Deschene, Lori. http://tinybuddha.com/blog/4-myths-about-doing-what-you-love-for-work/. Web. 15 Mar 2017

Eckart Tolle Describes Two Simple Exercises to Help You Live In The Now (VIDEO) http://www.huffingtonpost.com/2014/03/25/eckhart-tolle-a-new-earth-exercises-present- now_n_5024829.html

Emmons, R.A. & McCullough, M.E. (2003). Counting Blessings Versus Burdens: An Experimental Investigation of Gratitude and Subjective Well-Being in Daily Life. *Journal of Personality and Social Psychology*, Vol 84, No. 377-389

Foundation for Inner Peace. *A Course in Miracles*, Volume One Text. Coleman Graphics, Eight Printing, December 1984, Print

Gawain, Shakti. *Creative Visualization*. Nataraj Publishing, 1978, Print Goal Setting Research. http://happierhuman.com/goal-setting-research/

Goddard, Neville, *Awakened Imagination*, n.p., PDF

APPENDIX

Gregoire, S., Bouffard, T., Vezeau, C. (2012). Personal goal setting as mediator of the relationship between mindfulness and wellbeing. International Journal of Wellbeing, 2(3), 236-250. Doi:10.5502/ijw.v2.i3.5

Hicks, Jerry and Ester. *Ask and It is Given.* Hay House, Inc. 2004, Print

Holy Bible: King James Version, Web

Holy Bible: New International Version, Web

"If You Can't Imagine, How Can You Learn?". https://www.theguardian.com/education/2016/jun/04/aphantasia-no-visual-imagination-impact-learning. Web 2 Feb 2017

Isaac, A. R. (1992). Mental Practice- Does it Work in the Field? The Sport Psychologist, 6, 192-198. Healthpsych.Psy.Vanderbuild.edu/HealthPsych/mentalimagery.html. Web. 30 Jan 2017.

Jeannerod, M. (1994). Mental Imagery in the Motor Context. http://citeseerx.ist.psu.edu/viewdoc/download?doi=10.1.1.120.6640&rep=rep1&type=pdf. Web, 31 Jan. 2017.

Kabat-Zinn, Jon. (1979). An Outpatient Program in Behavioral Medicine for Chronic Pain Patients Based on the Practices of Mindfulness Meditation: Theoretical Considerations and Preliminary Results.

Matthews, Gail. Goal Research Summary. http://www.dominican.edu/academics/ahss/undergraduate-programs/psych/faculty/assets-gail-matthews/researchsummary2.pdf. Web, 1 Mar 2017

Masters, Paul Leon. *Master's Degree Curriculum.* 2 vols. Burbank, CA: Burbank Printing, 2012. Print.

--- Ministers/Bachelor Curriculum. 4 Vols. Burbank, CA: Burbank Printing, 2012. PDF File. Merriam-Webster Dictionary, Web

Most People have Unwanted, Worrying thoughts – Live Science. http://www.livescience.com/44687-most-people-have-unwanted-thoughts.

html. Web 16 Mar 2017

Nolen-Hoeksema, S., Wisco, B., Lyuboirsky,S. (1991). Rethinking Rumination. Perspectives on Psychological Science.

Patent, Arnold, M. *You Can Have It All: A Simple Guide to a Joyful and Abundant Life.* Good Times Books Pvt. Ltd/Celebration Publishing, 2013, Print.

---*The Journey.* Celebration Publishing, 2010, Print.

"Physics and Consciousness, Quantum Interconnectedness, Nature of Mind, Body and Spirit." Starstuffs.com/physcon/science.html. Web, 30 Jan. 2017

Pruyser, Paul. *The Minister as Diagnostician: Personal Problems in Pastoral Perspective.* Westminster Press, 1976, Print

Robbins, Tony. *Awaken the Giant Within: How to Take Immediate Control of Your Mental, Emotional and Physical and Financial Destiny.* Free Press, 1991, Print.

Savelle, Jerry. The Battle between Your Ears. Web. http://www.cfaith.com/index.php/blog/36-articles/christmas/15653-the-battle-is-between-your-ears. Web 31 Jan. 2017

Self-Pity: 11 Tell-Tale Signs That You're Self-Inflicted Victim. https://lonerwolf.com/self- pity/. Web 3 Mar 2017

DeSteno, David (2014). Gratitude: A Tool for Reducing Economic Impatience. Psychological Science 2014, Vol 25(6) 1262-1267).

"Successful People who use the Power of Visualization". MindBodyGreen.com. http://www.mindbodygreen.com/0-20630/8-successful-people-who-use-the-power-of- visualization.html. Web 31 Jan. 2017

"The Third Universal Truth: Everything is Connected." FindingtheField.com. Web, 30 Jan. 2017

APPENDIX

Tolle, Eckhart. *The Power of Now.* Namaste Publishing, 1999. PDF

22 Mindfulness Exercises, Techniques & Activities for Adults (+PDF's) https://positivepsychologyprogram.com/mindfulness-exercises-techniques-activities/ 20 Mar 2017

US San Diego News Center http://ucsdnews.ucsd.edu/pressrelease/u.s._media_consumption_to_rise_to_15.5_hours_a_day_per_person_by_2015. Web 19 Mar 2017

Wallace, B. Alan. M*inding Closely, The Four Applications of Mindfulness.* Snow Lion Publication. 2011, PDF

Whipple, M., Lewis, T., Sutton-Tyrell, K., Matthews, K. Barinas-Mitchell, E. Powell, L., Everson-Rose, S. Hopelessness, Depressive Symptoms, and Carotid Atherosclerosis in Women. 2009 Oct;40(10):3166-72. doi: 10.1161/STROKEAHA.109.554519. Epub 2009 Aug 27.

Why Ruminating is Unhealthy and How to Stop https://psychcentral.com/blog/archives/2011/01/20/why-ruminating-is-unhealthy-and-how-to-stop/. Web. 12 Mar 2017

Wilson-Coleman, *Is Anybody Listening: A Journey to Wholeness.* Champagne Connection, 2001, Print.
--- *Embracing Life's Lessons.* The Champagne Connection. 2004, Print
--- *Be Sure You Dance: Life's Lessons to help you make every moment count.* The Champagne Connection. 2010, Print

ABOUT THE AUTHOR

STEPHANIE E. WILSON-COLEMAN, PH.D. lives her inspiration as the Founder and CEO of The Champagne Connection, Inc. She is the author of four published inspirational books. Her fourth book, Creating a Masterpiece from a MasterMess, provides keys to use your "Super Powers" to change your life. Stephanie is the host of the popular cable access television show A Sip of Inspiration.

Everybody has a story and Stephanie's life narrative is a testament that anyone can have a story worth telling. Her story is filled with conflict, villains, roadblocks, moral dilemmas and spiritual awakenings.

Stephanie's story began in Little Rock, Arkansas, where she graduated at the top of her class from the historic Little Rock Central High School. She managed to do this in spite of becoming a mother at 15, experiencing sexual abuse and attending high school in the midst of intense racial tension. She beat the odds. Several years ago, an accident caused Stephanie to suffer a basal skull fracture from which the doctors predicted she would not recover. Again, she beat the odds. After recovering from the basal skull fracture, Stephanie, a victim of corporate downsizing, was left in financial ruin, which resulted in being temporarily homeless. And again, she beat the odds.

The same drive that led her to complete high school with honors, led Stephanie to earn her bachelor's degree at the University of Arkansas and a MBA from the University of Chicago's Executive MBA program. She even studied economics and finance in Singapore and Barcelona, Spain, which created her desire to travel the world and experience other cultures. Stephanie has visited more than 7 countries. She has also received a Ph.D., specializing in Holistic Life Coaching, from the University of Sedona, and a bachelor and master degree in Metaphysical Science from the University of Metaphysics. She is an ordained Metaphysical Minister, having received her ordination and practitioner

ABOUT THE AUTHOR

diploma from the International Metaphysical Ministry University Seminary.

Stephanie, a Success Mindset Mentor & Transformational Specialist and Pranic Healing Enthusiast, has the uncanny ability to help others transform emotional and mental obstacles into stepping stones to living their dreams. She has an insatiable appetite for helping others rethink the impossible. A few minutes with Stephanie is intoxicating. She effortlessly mesmerizes and inspires audiences. Whether she is engaging a small group, doing one-on-one mentoring/counseling, speaking at a large conference or presenting from a pulpit, everyone will experience a breakthrough.

Her superpower: Transforming Lives. With her guidance, teeth-rattling, soul shaking experience vaporize at her command.

Exhorting others to "live the life you imagine," Stephanie helps others talk about, identify, and work to resolve the difficult, emotional, and often painful behavior and actions that affect their financial health and the financial health of their families. By uncovering the memories that are keeping others chained to old worn out stories of failure. Sometimes called the "Straight No-Chaser Motivator," Stephanie is able to help others embrace the change required to alter their lives.

Stephanie shares an inspirational and life-changing message through her company's workshops, seminars, books, CDs, videos and other speaking engagements. As a Transformational Specialist, she has given people the tools needed to not only live their dreams and finally start "that business," but to also lead movements in their cities that have dramatically changed the lives of others.

One of Stephanie's core principles is to be of service to others. The businesses she has coached have not only changed the lives of others but have also increased their revenues by as much as 150%. If you're on the brink of disaster, Stephanie is the lifeline you should reach out to.

Driven by the beliefs that every day is a miracle and that stamina, discipline and strength are necessary companions, Stephanie facilitates

ABOUT THE AUTHOR

an annual **Ignite Your Inner Millionaire** conference, designed to help others change their mindset in order to achieve success. The seminar topics are critical to those whose dreams have been deferred by the mountains in their lives; e.g. poverty, abuse, teenage parenting, etc., but still have a strong desire to achieve something great in their lifetime.

For her outstanding contributions to the community, Stephanie received the Diamond Spirit Award in 2014, the Crescent Moon Award and the Minnie Riperton Humanitarian Award in 2013, the Dyvine Destiny Phenomenal Woman Award in 2012, the Chicago Defender's Women of Excellence Award and The Verizon Hometown Heroes Award in 2011 and The Black Pearl Award in 2005. She is actively involved with homeless shelters, at-risk youth, teenage mothers and victims of domestic violence.

Stephanie's truism: "We can't always control how our story begins, but we can write ourselves a better ending. Life's too short to drink cheap champagne."

For more information visit www.champagneconnection.com

www.facebook.com/empowerdr
www.facebook.com/empowermentmentdoctor
www.twitter.com/empowerdr
www.linkedin.com/empowerdr

Get your free copy of Blueprint to Financial Success to help you identify the hidden triggers that are derailing your financial success.
https://champagneconnection.com/blueprint/

P O BOX 87468, Chicago IL 60680.

DreamBig@champagneconnection.com

www.ingramcontent.com/pod-product-compliance
Lightning Source LLC
Chambersburg PA
CBHW051101160426
43193CB00010B/1272